In Praise of America's Collectors

In Praise of America's Collectors

Their Secrets Reveal
How to Be a Successful Collector

Arthur Warren Schultz

Santa Barbara Museum of Art
1130 State Street
Santa Barbara, CA 93101

© 1997 by Arthur Warren Schultz.
All rights reserved. No part of this publication may be transmitted in any form by any means, electronic or mechanical, including photocopy, recording, or any storage and retrieval system, without prior written permission from the publisher.

Printed in the United States of America
Published and distributed by the Santa Barbara Museum of Art

Edited by Beverly Fazio Herter
Designed by Nanette Boyer

Photographers: Thomas Cinoman, p.132 (top)
Robert Gray, p.132 (bottom)
David Heald, p.134 (top)
SFMOMA/Richard Barnes, p. 134 (middle)
Alex Vertikoff, p.134 (bottom)

Library of Congress Cataloging-in-Publication Data

Schultz, Arthur W.
In Praise of America's Collectors/by Arthur W. Schultz.
p. cm.
Includes bibliographical references and index.
ISBN 0-89951-099-X
1. Collectors and collecting–United States I. Title.
AM303.S38 1998
381'.45002'0973-dc21   98-12326
                                    CIP

Cover:

William F. Draper. *Paul Mellon*, 1974, oil on canvas. Paul Mellon Collection, National Gallery of Art, Washington. © Board of Trustees, National Gallery of Art, Washington.

Edward Steichen, *Portrait of Gertrude Vanderbilt Whitney*, 1937, gelatin silver print. Collection of Whitney Museum of American Art, Gift of the family of Edith and Lloyd Goodrich. © 1997 Whitney Museum of American Art.

Pierpont Morgan, 1902. Courtesy of the Archives, The Pierpont Morgan Library, New York.

Table of Contents

Acknowledgements   page vii
Foreword   page ix
Introduction   page x

Chapter 1   A National Phenomenon –   page 3
               Created by America's Collectors

Chapter 2   The Beginning of It All –   page 11
               How the American Collector Launched
               the Greatest Museum System

Chapter 3   The Power of an Idea –   page 30
               How a Banker, a Merchant, a Stockbroker, a
               Teacher and a Butcher Changed the
               Museum World

Chapter 4   Why People Collect –   page 40
               Secrets of the Great Collectors

Chapter 5   How To Start a Collection –   page 47
               Key Steps to Collecting Without Heartache

Chapter 6   The Cardinal Rules for Collecting -   page 52
               How To Become a Successful Collector
               Even If You Are Not Rich

Chapter 7   A Few True Heroes and Heroines –   page 58
               The Amateur Collectors Who Created Our
               Cultural, Artistic and Historic Institutions

Chapter 8   Collecting for History –   page 80
               How Our Most Important Presidential Sites
               Were Saved

Chapter 9	Unusual Collectors and Collections – The Passions and Acquisitions of Some Unconventional Americans	page 87
Chapter 10	Fascinating Characters – Paragons and Miscreants of the Collecting World	page 103
Chapter 11	The Importance of Dealers – How To Deal with the Middlemen	page 112
Photographs		page 115
Chapter 12	Lord Joseph Duveen – The "Babe Ruth" of Art Dealers	page 126
Chapter 13	The Value of Auction Houses – How To Buy at Auctions Wisely and Without Fear	page 135
Chapter 14	Fakes, Forgeries, Copies, Stolen Goods and Other Problems – How To Keep from Being Cheated	page 139
Chapter 15	The Economics – Collecting for Pleasure and Profit	page 155
Chapter 16	Things That People Collect – From Advertising to Zodiacs	page 169
Chapter 17	Predictions – Thoughts for a New Millennium	page 174
Appendix	Institutions Named for Collectors	page 176
Bibliography		page 182

Acknowledgements

SO MANY PEOPLE contributed to this book over the years by sharing their knowledge and experiences with me. Without exception, they were generous with their time, ideas and enthusiasm and gave of their energy and efforts unstintingly. Their dedication and the examples they set added immensely to my life.

At the Art Institute of Chicago, Marshall Field, Arthur M. Wood, James and Marilyn Alsdorf, Stanley M. Freehling, Brooks McCormick, John H. Bryan, Bryan S. Reid, Jr., Leigh and Mary Block, James N. Wood, Robert E. Mars, Larry Ter Molen, Judy Spies, Marija Raudys, Jack P. Brown, Katherine Lee, James Speyer, Harold Joachim, Suzanne F. McCullagh, Courtney G. Donnell, David B. Travis, Christa C. Thurman, Milo Naeve.

Members of President Reagan's and Bush's President's Committee on the Arts and the Humanities Andrew Heiskell, Donald J. Hall, Armand S. Deutch, J. Carter Brown, Robert McCormick Adams, Joan Kent Dillon, Diane J. Paton, James H. Billington, Daniel J. Boorstin, Lynne V. Cheney, Roger L. Stevens, Lloyd E. Cotsen, Franklin D. Murphy, Schuyler G. Chapin, S. Dillon Ripley, Leonard L. Silverstein—and especially Nancy Reagan and Barbara Bush who were our Honorary Chairs.

At Heritage Preservation (previously the National Institute for the Conservation of Cultural Property) and the American Institute for Conservation Lawrence L. Reger, Ross Merrill, Carolyn L. Rose, William R. Leisher, Inge-lise Eckmann, Elizabeth A. C. Perry, Debbie Hess Norris, Arthur Beale, Joyce Hill Stoner, Terry Drayman-Weisser, Jane Long, Sarah Rosenberg and Paul Gottlieb and Harriet Whelchel of Abrams.

At the Santa Barbara Museum of Art Paul and Leslie Ridley-Tree, Eli and Leatrice Luria, Robert K. and Barbara Straus, John and Zola Rex, Mercedes Eichholz, Austin H. and Jean Peck, Jr., James P. and Stanya

Owen, Lorna Hedges, Otto Wittmann, Priscilla Giesen, Michael G. Wilson, Jon B. and Lillian Lovelace, Barbara Bradley, Ernest Clark, Jr., Willard G. DeGroot, Richard Reed Armstrong, Robert M. Light, J. Robert Andrews, Carol L. Valentine, J. Hewes Crispin, Herbert R. Peterson, F. Bailey Vanderhoef, Jr., Robert M. and Anne Jones, Paul N. Perrot, Robert H. Frankel, Barbara B. Luton, Ron Crozier, Deborah Borrowdale-Cox, Diana du Pont, Susan Tai, Karen Sinsheimer, Cherie Summers, Terry Atkinson, Kathy O'Leary, Shelley Ruston, Penny Mast McCall, Kelly Cretti, John Coplin.

At the University of Chicago Edward H. Levi, Hannah H. Gray, Hugo F. Sonnenschein, James H. Douglas, Edwin A. and Lindy Bergman, J. Parker Hall II, Alice D. Schreyer, Randy Holgate, Jonathan Kleinbard, Fairfax M. Cone, Gaylord Donnelley, Robert W. Reneker, Edward W. Rosenheim, John E. Jeuck, Jonathan Z. Smith, Stuart M. Tave.

In several related activities and projects—Harold M. Williams, Daniel J. Terra, Jack Adams, Jane Sienna Talley, Luis Monreal, Earl A. Powell III, Peter C. Marzio, Elizabeth Rauh Pulitzer, Peter G. Sparks, John L. Marion, Huntington T. Block, Steven Weintraub, Margaret Holben Ellis, Doris A. Hamburg, Brian Considine, Sara J. Wolf, Meg Craft, George Segan Wheeler, J. Scott Odell, Wilbur Faulk, Richard Newman, Shelley G. Sturman, Barry R. Bauman.

And in actually putting this book together Cathy Pollock, Beverly Fazio Herter, Nanette Boyer, Harold E. Schultz, Dixie Bahr, Cynthia K. Schultz and my devoted and always encouraging wife Susan.

To each and every one, more thanks than I know how bestow.

*To the dedicated and generous collectors who gave us
the marvelous museums we all treasure and enjoy so much—
and to those who will follow.*

– *Arthur W. Schultz*

Foreword

In Praise of American Collectors provides a fascinating history of private collecting, and traces the remarkable influence of individual collectors on the development of American museums. It seems particularly appropriate that the Santa Barbara Museum of Art serve as publisher for this book, as our collections directly reflect the importance of private collectors. Over ninety percent of the works housed here have been gifts from individuals. A broad spectrum of collectors who lived in our area or who became aware of the richness of the holdings of the Museum have, through their generous donations of art, allowed us to share their passion with all who visit.

As Arthur Schultz notes in his book, the evolution of this institution mirrors that of many others in the United States. Gifts—from collections first put together for private enjoyment, or purchased specifically to augment an existing public collection—form the core of American museums.

Arthur Schultz, through his long involvement with the arts, has, in fact, become a collector himself—a collector of information about museums and the people responsible for their development, and of advice and suggestions for both the casual and the more dedicated collector. In this book, he contributes that information to the public, communicating at the same time his own love of objects and of arts organizations, in the time-honored manner of important collectors throughout history.

– Robert H. Frankel
Director, Santa Barbara Museum of Art

Introduction

"Which man is the happier—He that hath a collection of unexcelled quality and quantity or he who has thirteen daughters? The happier man is the man with thirteen daughters because he knows that he has enough. The collector, on the other hand, is never satisfied. He would not be a true collector otherwise."
– Philip Hofer, Harvard's greatest book donor

"There is no average collector."
– John Walker, former director of the National Gallery of Art

THE IDEA FOR THIS BOOK was a long time coming. While my business life was spent in communications, advertising, marketing and newspapering, my other life has been spent in the cultural and educational areas, particularly since retirement. In that life I was the lay head of two art museums and a trustee of my alma mater. Then Presidents Reagan and Bush appointed me to their Committees for the Arts and Humanities and I was elected a director of the National Institute for the Conservation of Cultural Property and served on the advisory committee of the American Institute for Conservation of Artistic and Historic Works. With time I came to realize the tremendous impact collectors have had on our educational and cultural institutions and how often, in the rush of time and activities, the value of their contributions can be underappreciated, unknown or even lost. By invitation, I delivered a few addresses on the importance of collectors, relating some of their dazzling contributions. The audiences were as moved by these generous individuals as I had been and yearned to learn more—particularly as to how and why collectors had created their collections and then contributed them to museums, libraries and other institutions of their choice. For most of the audience, the stories were new and the impact of the collectors on their lives realized for the first time.

I next reviewed the literature on the subject of collectors and collecting. There is a paucity compared to the high volume of art books. Most of what has been written was published two, three and four decades ago. Among these volumes, many dealt with the individual collector's personal idiosyncrasies and dedicated most of the pages to describing the collections in detail and color, concentrating on the objects rather than the collector. Slight attention is paid to the motivation for assembling or how the collectors dispensed their collections. For these reasons, I decided to tell the magnificent story of the American collector in a compact, easy-to-read form with the hope that it will stimulate many of us to take up this noble avocation, or, for those already addicted, to think seriously of sharing our pleasures and treasures with the people.

Collecting is the most popular leisure time activity in America. More people collect objects of all descriptions than play golf and tennis combined. Or than buy tickets to all the professional sport games in total. Or than have ever attended college. Most of us spend more time collecting every day than we do reading the daily newspaper. The number of people collecting increases 10 percent a year and will continue to do so as the babyboomers reach their fifties, the years when enthusiasm for collecting replaces more mundane interests.

Indeed, we Americans lavish more on adding to our collections and giving them away so that others may enjoy them than is spent on any other leisure-time activity.

Each of us carries the collector's gene. Each of us is the beneficiary of the collecting passions of others although that fact may be lost to us as we scurry through our chores and the challenges of life.

A casual stroll through our homes is moving testimony. The art on our walls may have first appealed to our ancestors. The art we succumb to will, in turn, very likely grace our children's and grandchildren's homes in years to come. The furniture we live with may have been our parents. Those pieces we purchased will become familiar to our children, and, as they become attached to them, chances are high that they will find their way into their future homes. After a generation or two they may even graduate to the heirloom category. If our selections or those of our parents were choice to begin with, these pieces will undoubtedly increase in value with the passage of time. The books in our homes that beckon to us include those we grew up with as children in our parents' houses.

So by chance or by choice we are both the inheritors who have benefited from the selection and care of others and the progenitors for still another generation.

Almost everyone collects something. It may be family pictures. To some personal items are the most precious of all. Buffalo Bill Cody, on being notified that his house was on fire, said, "Save my portrait, let the house burn." It had been painted by Rosa Bonheur in Paris, and he cherished it. Others still save coins and stamps from collections started as children, fine paintings or baseball cards, antique cars or thimbles or books, as the author does. The number of things people can and do collect is virtually endless. We have a genius for expanding our imaginations. Further on in the book you will find a listing of hundreds of areas that have attracted collecting interest.

Yet with all this activity, involvement and investment in collecting, it does not appear that a single college or university offers a program on collecting, let alone a course. Nor am I familiar with a museum whose educational agenda invites members and others to a course or instruction on collecting. This is particularly arresting since museums are the constant beneficiaries of collectors. There are only a scattering of programs on public television and cable stations that deal with collecting. Publishers issue hundreds of books on art but few, if any, on how to build a collection, except in very specialized fields. Despite this lack of formal training and education, millions of people consider themselves collectors and please themselves and others with their accomplishments. Because they are often extravagant with their time, they gradually learn in a rather hit-or-miss manner the right way to approach collecting.

Hopefully, this book will help collectors expand their abilities to build collections and enhance the excitement that collecting can bring to us. It offers advice and suggestions to the person who is just starting to build a collection as well as to those who are much further along. The beginner will save time, money and effort and avoid the many common mistakes and errors novices invariably commit, and the veteran collector will value the book's many anecdotes and perhaps be moved to join the ranks of the generous characters featured in its pages—America's great collectors.

In Praise of America's Collectors

Chapter 1

A NATIONAL PHENOMENON – CREATED BY AMERICA'S COLLECTORS

"The astonishing growth of American Museums, in both size and numbers, is a phenomenon unique in the world because it has come about almost entirely through the generosity of private citizens."
— Germain Seligman, international art dealer

"America's cathedrals are her museums."
— Andrè Malraux, French historian and cultural leader

"A trip to the United States today is like a tour of Italy in the eighteenth century."
— Pierre Cabanne, art historian and author

THIS BOOK IS IN PRAISE of American collectors, the magnificent museums and institutions they created and the lessons they have learned in pursuing their passions that can now be shared by all of us who are similarly driven. As one art historian put it, "America's museums have become our privileged places. They are local, national and international. They store and reveal beauty, wealth, pride and powerful egos. Most of all, they please and educate all of us and particularly our children."

As a collector, you are a member of a group of benefactors who have had a tremendous impact on our lives and our understanding of history. Unlike so many collectors in other countries, who collect primarily or exclusively for their own financial benefit and private pleasure, a large number of American collectors, through their generosity in giving to our institutions for all to enjoy, have performed an extravagant service to our country.

Collectors are the most important group for the founding of American museums and the preservation of our cultural history. Many institutions are named for the persons who founded them to house their collections (see Appendix). Collectors are also recognized with the naming of galleries, special exhibition rooms and buildings. While a few museums such as Toledo, Cleveland, Kimball and, of course, the Getty, have acquired much of their collections through acquisitions, over 90 percent of all objects contained in our museums arrived there as gifts from collectors. The value of a museum's holdings far exceeds the value of its physical plant—often by one hundred times or more. And the value of the collections continue to grow each year. People naturally visit museums primarily to see the collections, but the skills of directors, curators and architects have contributed greatly to our overall experience as they design beautiful areas in which we may view the collections.

It may not be too great an exaggeration to claim that without collectors there would be no museums in America, no professional staffs to manage and operate our museums, no art educational programs, no exhibitions, no art magazines or art books. For this reason it appears odd that the *Official Museum Directory*, which is two thousand pages thick and lists more than seven thousand institutions, includes only a handful of founders of museums as such. Clearly this is the most important person in the history of each institution. For example, the listing for the Field Museum of Natural History in Chicago runs over 350 words yet never mentions that Marshall Field was the founder. I realize this may not be the primary purpose of the directory, but it is important information and more than matches some of the other material carried for interest. I'm fearful that this absence may be interpreted as reflecting a rather low regard for the history of the institution and a lack of appreciation for the donor-collector who made this great institution available to the public. As a graduate and trustee of the University of Chicago, I am always pleased to note that John D. Rockefeller is acclaimed the founder on all official stationary. Perhaps this book will help restore our appreciation for the people who made the first step and founded so many of our institutions.

Collectors are part of this most vital constituency to our nation's desire to preserve its cultural heritage. As a collector, or someone with the desire to be one, you, too, can play an important role in preserving the history of America and become a part of it.

Corporations often become collectors. They consider it good business, believing that the public and employees feel such investments reflect their interest in our country by preserving and conserving important cultural, historic and artistic icons. It increases their visibility, heightens their image, boosts morale and may improve productivity. On occasion, collections have been sold in times of financial stress and have proved beneficial. Of *Fortune* magazine's annual listing of the top five hundred corporations, over half have collections of art, cultural or historic items that reflect their business's interests. The Campbell Soup Company created the outstanding collection of soup tureens from around the world that they recently gave to the Winterthur Museum. The Corning Glass Company founded the Museum of Glass, the superior collection on every aspect of glass history, along with a library. The Wells Fargo Bank maintains a history museum featuring stagecoaches, early mining equipment and the bank's history. The IBM corporation built an art collection equal to that of many museums. The Atchison, Topeka & Santa Fe railroad had a dazzling collection of western art capturing that part of our country that the Santa Fe services. The Eli Lilly Company maintains a pharmacology museum in Indianapolis. The Levi Strauss company, makers of Levi's blue jeans, has a museum dealing with the company's history and the opening of the west. It recently received a hundred-year-old pair of Levis found in a dry, abandoned mine. Atlantic Richfield and the First Chicago Bank have long had fine art collections. The John Deere Company maintains an historical agricultural museum in Moline, Illinois, and preserves the home of its founder. Motorola opened a museum on the evolution of the electronics industry at its headquarters in Illinois.

Clubs also collect. Members often leave them objects. The Union League Club in Chicago has an outstanding art collection, which is added to by members; Los Angeles's California Club is also justly proud of its art collection. Clubs assemble historic memorabilia pertaining to their members' activities. They feel these collections add to the pleasure their members find at the club and create an appearance of solidarity and well-being. There is nothing to match the silver awards and ship models exhibited by the New York Yacht Club. Collections may also serve as a reserve when needed. A club in Santa Barbara that owned a Remington painting sold it through auction to obtain needed funds for renovation of the club; but first they had a copy made.

People love to collect. Douglas Cooper, a distinguished professor of fine arts at the University of Oxford, summed up the appeal by observing, "The urge to collect has revealed itself throughout history as a fundamentally human phenomenon." A recent national survey estimated that more than 22 million Americans are amassing collectibles such as dolls, knives, figurines and plates. They spent an amazing $8 billion on these and other collectibles in 1995. This is probably just the beginning as the babyboomers are starting to reach the most active collecting ages of forty-five to sixty-five. A majority of Americans take photographs regularly, and 75 percent of them keep their pictures in albums. We have all heard stories of disasters such as floods, fires, earthquakes occurring and the residents rushing in to save their photo albums before anything else. These are precious mementos of a family's life and times and cannot be replaced.

It is reasonable to assume, although statistics are not available, that collectors in America outnumber all those in Europe—

perhaps the world. Since the turn of the century, America has spent more on building, maintaining, expanding and filling its museums and cultural institutions with the treasures of the world than all other countries combined.

This phenomenon grew out of the very character of America as compared with the countries in the old world. James Wood, president and director of the Art Institute of Chicago, suggests that our drive for history and identity is central to the American experience, as is our obsession with and respect for the individual. Historically, the responsibility for the preservation of cultural, artistic and historical objects fell upon the nobility, the aristocracy and the Church. Private collections were unknown in classical Greece—everything was public property, including their precious libraries. The Greeks treasured books. Cleopatra learned from them and presided over the great library at Alexandria. The early Egyptian royal families were prodigious collectors, stuffing their tombs with furniture, jewelry, toys, ointments, monuments, chariots and weapons for the deceased's afterlife. Tutankhamen's tomb released the combined objects of several Pharaohs and may have been the largest collection ever assembled. Our museums now contain many items recovered from tombs more than four thousand years old.

Rome, on the other hand, encouraged private collections. There was such a surfeit of "liberated" works from conquered peoples that forty libraries were established; works of art were plentiful enough to fill a score of museums. Caesar's collection of cameos was renowned: some of his booty may still be seen in the Louvre and the Hermitage. Pompeii's bronze *Hercules* is in the Vatican. One report put it that Rome had as many statues as citizens.

Then after the fall of the Roman empire, an uneasy quiet settled over Europe, lasting a thousand years. Little, if any, collecting was evidenced. The Church in early medieval Europe hoarded and hid treasures and manuscripts and took extraordinary measures to keep them from the barbarians. The monks were so secretive and possessive about their books that they at times chained them to the bookshelves. Daniel Boorstin, the Librarian of Congress Emeritus, notes in his book *The Discoverers* that one monk went so far as to write in a manuscript, "This book belongs to the monastery of St. Mary of Robert's Bridge, whoever shall steal it from this house or mutilate it let him be forever cursed. Amen." Whatever one may think about their methods, there is no doubt that the monks were responsible for saving what was left of the ancient cultures after the barbarians had leveled the empire.

Objects and art of the medieval period are among the most valued today. John D. Rockefeller, Jr., built and endowed the Cloisters in New York City as a branch of the Metropolitan Museum of Art to house such works. A director of the Louvre observed, "The Cloisters is the crowning achievement of American museology."

The Medici family led the way out of the abyss as they initiated private collecting again. They collected treasures for nearly four hundred years before Anna Maria Luisa, known as "the last of the Medici," bequeathed the entire Medici collection to the city of Florence, "for the utility of the people and to attract the curiosity of foreigners," in 1743. Thus the Uffizi was converted from the Medici's princely art gallery to the first truly public museum. The Medici collected massively—pictures, statues (including Michelangelo's creations), gems, bronzes, busts, coins, cameos, libraries, armor, arms, Egyptian antiquities, tapestries, furniture, gold and silver objects, china, carvings and clothes.

Popes over the ages have been prodigious collectors. However, until the eighteenth century, the popes considered their collections their own personal property and frequently left them to relatives, who in turn, more often than not, sold them. Foreign buyers flocked to Rome to take advantage of this turnover, and countless treasures left the Vatican and Rome. Indeed, the collections were being liquidated so rapidly that the popes finally felt compelled to change policy and the laws. The popes' collections now belonged to the Church, and strict laws were passed to forbid the export of antiquities.

Simultaneously the popes expanded their search for antiquities and increased their acquisitions. Master artists commissioned to create special works for the Vatican included Botticelli, Signorelli, Perugino, Verrochio, Giorgione, Titian, Leonardo da Vinci, Michelangelo and Raphael. In 1503 the private collection of Pope Julius II entered the Vatican's first museum, to be followed by those of Clement VIII and Paul III. Museums and galleries continued to be built and expanded, and eventually the Vatican became the most comprehensive complex in the world at that time. It is mind-boggling to imagine all that would be housed within the Vatican today if the earlier popes had not distributed their booty as they did.

As private institutions, museums are about four hundred years old. Acquisitions by kings and queens during the Renaissance created the need to build secure areas in which to house their collections. While the first national institution established was the British Museum in 1759, by an act of Parliament, the real impetus for the idea of national galleries grew out of the French Revolution. In 1793, a year after the overthrow of the French monarchy, the Louvre was opened to the public. Former royal collections became the nuclei of the Hermitage, Dresden and Prado museums. With the final defeat of Napoleon, the victors returned many objects that had been stolen, and these became the centerpieces of national museums in Brussels, Milan and Amsterdam. The Louvre, however, still possesses some of Napoleon's plunder.

Public rather than private collections are the children of the Industrial Revolution. The National Gallery of London was founded in 1832 to assist English manufacturers in improving their design standards as they competed for overseas markets. The objects in these early museums grew in value and brought prestige to the nation; also, they helped educate and motivate the citizenry. With time, these public museums matched and then exceeded the holdings of the monarchs.

Royal families accumulated collections over generations and centuries, as some still do. The House of Windsor in England to this day probably controls the greatest private collection in the treasures it owns. Before the revolution, the kings of France through Louis XV amassed every describable object . The Louvre is a perfect example of how European museums came into being. Under Philippe Auguste the building of the Louvre as a fortress was started in 1190. In 1546 King Frances I, an art collector, converted these and other structures to house his ample art collection. Succeeding monarchs up to Louis XIV kept adding to the complex. Cardinals, including de Richelieu and Mazarin, acquired art properties for their kings, including King Charles I's collection after the British Parliament had him executed. The Louvre was finally opened to the public in 1793 after the Revolution. The expansion of the Louvre continues to this day. Recently 100,000 square feet of new gallery space was opened. All of the additions have been at government expense, the latest costing $1 billion over fifteen years. Annually the government provides $50 million to operate the Louvre. The House of Hapsburg ruled the Austro-Hungarian empire for over four hundred years until the end of World War I and rapaciously gathered in all that was available. They rivaled the popes as collectors. Museums in Madrid, Brussels and Vienna were the final beneficiaries. The Prado in Spain was founded by King Frederick VII in 1819 and holds much of the Royal collection. The Rijksmuseum, founded in 1800 in Amsterdam, contains major portions of the Royal collection. Similar backgrounds surround the Dresden Gallery, the Alexandria museum in Egypt and the British museum. All continue to be supported by their governments.

As you can imagine, the general public had no access to these royal compounds. As one scholar observed, "The European ruling classes didn't need museums, they lived in them."

Chapter 2

THE BEGINNING OF IT ALL – HOW THE AMERICAN COLLECTOR LAUNCHED THE GREATEST MUSEUM SYSTEM

"The collector is willing and eager to have others share his pleasure. It is for this reason I established my museum."
– J. Paul Getty

"American museums are universities for the general public – institutions dedicated to the learning and enrichment of all."
– Germain Bazin, former chief curator of the Louvre

AMERICA'S EXPERIENCE has been quite different from that of Europe. Whereas foreign nations have pursued collecting for centuries, starting with the private collections of their royal families and aristocracy, America's first recorded effort to save and preserve a few of our historically significant objects was the formation of A Library Society in Charleston, South Carolina, in 1773. In 1791 the Massachusetts Historical Society was founded, followed by the American Academy of Fine Arts in New York in 1802, the New York Historical Society in 1804, the Pennsylvania Academy of the Fine Arts in 1805, Baltimore's Peale Museum in 1814 and the Trumbull Gallery at Yale University in

1832. The Wadsworth Atheneum in Hartford, Connecticut, most often acknowledged to be our first museum, opened in 1844. Finally, in 1846, Congress established the Smithsonian Institution in response to a handsome cash gift by James Smithson. It wasn't until five years after the Civil War that our major cities began founding museums. The Metropolitan Museum of Art in New York, Boston's Museum of Fine Arts and the Corcoran Gallery of Art in Washington, D.C., were each founded in 1870. They were followed by the Philadelphia Museum of Art in 1876, the Worcester Art Museum in Massachusetts and the Art Institute of Chicago in 1893. Before these dates, the citizens in these cities had no place to view or study fine art, natural history objects and scientific materials.

With the exception of the Smithsonian, for which Congress agreed to provide the operating costs in return for Smithson's founding gift, all of the above were organized by citizens as not-for-profit institutions to be managed by private boards. (Even the Smithsonian is sustained by private collectors and contributors. The most recent was a $20 million gift from Kenneth Behring; it was his way of saying "thank you" to America for all the opportunities it gave him.) They were created by local initiatives and retained private control—a good thing, too, since our local and federal governments have always been penurious when it comes to acquiring and supporting the arts and other cultural efforts. While some state and local governments do own museums, the holdings are from the private collector.

The federal government refused to buy Benjamin Franklin's library; as a result, Franklin's grandson sold it piecemeal and it has been largely lost track of. Similarly, the government declined to purchase George Washington's library from his heirs. Private citizens in Boston raised the necessary funds, and his library now rests in the Boston Athenaeum, one of our nation's finest libraries. The country nearly lost Thomas Jefferson's fine library as well. The government reluctantly agreed to purchase it only after the British burned the Library of Congress in the

War of 1812 and the national library was left without books. Buying Jefferson's collection was a quick fix.

The National Health Museum, founded in 1862 by the Defense Department, is located at the Walter Reed Army Medical Center in Washington, D. C. Although it contains such interesting pieces as the bullet that killed Abraham Lincoln and the dental instruments used by Paul Revere, very few people visit the museum because of its inaccessible location. Now a public drive is being launched to raise funds so as to relocate the museum to the mall where millions of people visit each year.

The Library of Congress, originally founded for the exclusive use of Congress when it was housed in the Capitol, outgrew that limited function and moved into its own permanent building in 1897. Congress still provides all the funds, and the library is the premier such institution in the world.

In the course of the development of this movement through the stimulation of private entrepreneurship, governments at the local, state and the federal level gradually came to realize how popular these institutions were. Voters urged cooperation from governments. Consequently, over the years, some have come to provide partial funds for operations and maintenance. Still, the latest data show that the majority of these funds are supplied from private sources. And, of course, private sources remain responsible for new buildings and additions and, most importantly, for creating and expanding the collections through gifts. The federal government, through allowing income tax deductions for gifts, may help stimulate donations to some degree. However, it remains that when an institution accepts a gift the cost to the donor is still substantial. He or she would be way ahead financially if the object were sold rather than given away. Also, in the early days when our major institutions were being founded, there was no income tax or it was minuscule. The founders gave generously without tax benefits in mind.

Recalling how the Metropolitan Museum of Art was founded in New York City will illustrate the pattern of organization that city after city followed in the years to come. The Metropolitan was organized by a small group of men, twenty-seven in all. The new board consisted of industrialists, financiers, railroaders, lawyers, a few city officials and four practicing artists.

As an example of how they intended to operate, in 1871, a year after the museum was founded, two trustees signed a bank loan in order to hold a collection the museum wished to acquire until they could pass the hat among all the trustees. They raised the necessary $100,000 without trouble. No governmental body was solicited. All this was so impressive that the city of New York eventually agreed to underwrite certain operational costs while private citizens were to be totally responsible for gathering the collections at no public expense. Other municipalities, as they recognized the tremendous value the new museums were bringing to the communities, participated in minimal ways with certain operational costs.

At the formal opening of the Metropolitan Museum, founding trustee Joseph C. Choate, a lawyer and future Ambassador to the Court of St. James, made these observations: "The Founders believe that diffusion of a knowledge of art in its higher forms of beauty will tend directly to humanize, to educate and to refine a practical and laborious people that thought great masterpieces could never be within their reach. The Founders thought it might be possible to gather together a collection of works of merit which should import some knowledge of art and its history to those who were yet to take almost their first steps in that department of knowledge." A few years later Choate addressed a group of New Yorkers in an attempt to get them to support the new museum. "Think of it, ye millionaires of many markets—what glory may be yours if you only listen to our advice, to convert pork to porcelain, grain and produce into priceless pottery, the rude ores of commerce into sculptured marble and railroad shares and mining stocks, things which perish without the using, and which in the next financial panic shall surely shrivel like parched scrolls, into the glorified canvas of the world's masters, that shall adorn these walls for centuries. The rage of Wall Street is to convert all baser things into gold, which is but dross. But ours is the higher ambition to convert useless gold into things of living beauty that shall be a joy to a whole people for a thousand years."

They responded. Who wouldn't? One of the world's greatest museums was on its way.

Enter J. P. Morgan, acknowledged at the time to be the premier banker and financier in the world. He wielded as much power in his area as a monarch. A large man with black eyes as sharp as bayonets, he would stare a person down until he received the answer and cooperation he sought. Few could stand up to him. He ruled the House of Morgan with absolute and total discretion; he demanded the best from everyone with whom he dealt. Yet he was loyal to those he respected and regarded character as more important than a strong financial balance sheet.

Although he did not start collecting in earnest until after his fiftieth birthday, Morgan moved so quickly and decisively that Francis Henry Taylor, a distinguished museum director in the 1940s and 50s, proclaimed him "the greatest figure in the art world that America has yet produced, a visionary and a patron such as we never saw before." He collected in the grand manner—only the best, and all the best that was available. In the next twenty-five years Morgan assembled the greatest collection in private hands. As a fellow trustee of the Metropolitan museum observed, "Morgan collected collections."

Because of his stature and accomplishments, Morgan transformed the Metropolitan. Other wealthy New York leaders became eager to join with him, and he marshaled their money and collections in support of his drive. Under his ten-year reign as president, the Metropolitan became America's leading museum and set standards for all others. In addition, he built an excellent staff. Morgan oversaw the finances as only he could, adding substantially to the museum's income and stability. He was determined to make the Metropolitan the world's finest museum.

Fine collections flowed to the museum simply by Morgan's asking for them and arranging appropriate deals. Few would think of turning Morgan down. One of his marvelous coups was having his fellow classmate from Harvard, William H. Riggs, an expatriate living in Paris, bequeath to the Metropolitan his entire collection of ancient arms and armor. At the time it was the finest in the world. In his letter to the museum making the assignment, Riggs stated he was doing this because of his fondness and respect for Morgan. It remains the outstanding collection of its type in America and is on permanent display to this day.

Morgan never bought American art, reasoning that it was already here. He wanted Americans to have the finest the world could offer and that meant buying the great art of Europe and the Middle East, which in his time was not available in America. He purchased jewels, carpets, tapestries, statues, paintings, armor, rock crystal, drawings, furniture, panels, snuff boxes, rare books—anything of artistic and historical value.

Morgan did everything in a regal manner. His annual buying trips to Europe, which lasted four to six months, were taken on his private yacht with a retinue of friends, experts, servants and staff. Wherever he went, an army of dealers awaited him. They brought to Morgan the very best they had to offer, having learned that because of his decisive way they would know quickly whether they had a sale. His acquisitions were prodigious.

At this time, the United States had prohibitive duty charges on imported works of art. Morgan owned a large home in London and had his acquisitions shipped there. He would face the duty at some future date. A year before his death, due in large part to his efforts, the law was changed to exempt works of art over one hundred years old. With that change, Morgan spent his last year packing up his treasures in London and shipping them to New York to be held in the basement of the museum. Morgan died in Rome shortly after they arrived in America but before they could be installed and exhibited at the Metropolitan. He was seventy-six years old.

The Beginning of It All

Today the Metropolitan Museum of Art is New York City's top tourist attraction.

The Metropolitan was not the only institution to be a beneficiary of Morgan's generosity. A large library adjoining his main residence in New York City housed his outstanding collection of rare books, over which his librarian Belle Greene held sway. After Morgan's death the residence and library combined to become the Pierpont Morgan Library and opened to the public. In recent years, due to continued acquisitions and donations, the library has completed a substantial addition. Morgan also left art and money to the Wadsworth Atheneum in Hartford, Connecticut, in memory of his father. The Morgan family had its roots in Hartford, and Morgan's gifts made the Wadsworth Atheneum a first-class museum.

Although Morgan relied heavily on the advice of experts in various fields such as porcelains, tapestries, bronzes and books, he never purchased anything he had not seen. Frequently he had dealers ship him objects on approval for months at a time. During this waiting period he would seek opinions from specialists. While he bought in large, often massive, quantities, there was nothing casual or slipshod about his disciplines.

By the time Morgan died in Rome, approximately half of his estate was in art—$60 million out of a $128 million total. These totals today would be in excess of a billion dollars. Because of this unbalance, the managers of his estate felt that some of his art holdings should be sold. As a result, about 40 percent was assigned to the Metropolitan and the rest went to market. Henry Clay Frick acquired some of the finest pieces, and they now reside in the Frick Collection mansion in New York. The British dealer Lord Joseph Duveen bought much of the balance and resold it to other collectors, several of whom eventually gave their collections to museums of their choice. In all, the Metropolitan and other museums reaped the harvest of J. P. Morgan's audacious and remarkable collecting, with the American people as the eternal beneficiaries.

Chicago's experience in establishing its museum complex was similar to New York's. As in the east, the initial citizen effort was to save their historical artifacts. The Chicago Historical Society was founded in 1856, followed quickly by the Academy of Sciences in 1857. It was the same growing desire on the part of leaders to bring culture to this still-frontier-style city that led them to form an art school in 1873 so that the "common folk" could begin to learn about art and art history and thus improve their lives. In this they were not unlike the England's upper classes in the Victorian era.

After a false start, a successful art school was launched in 1879. George Armour, the meat packer, was the first president. Levi Leiter, Marshall Field's partner, followed. And then young Charles Hutchinson took over. He was a successful banker and meat packer and served on several corporate boards. Hutchinson, along with his close associate and friend Martin Ryerson, presided over the new institution for more than thirty years. The response to the academy was so positive that an art museum followed in 1893, to be known as the Art Institute of Chicago. The academy still functions in association with the museum and is known as the School of the Art Institute; one of the largest and most successful in the nation, it serves more than two thousand students annually.

Hutchinson and Ryerson traveled to Europe annually and collected for the new museum many of the treasures that are still exhibited, including world class Old Masters and Impressionist paintings. Ryerson left more than three thousand works to the museum, many of which are still part of the core of the permanent collection. In addition, he willed the museum his book collection and funds to build and maintain the Martin Ryerson Art Library, one of the largest and finest in the world.

Marshall Field founded the Field Museum of Natural History in 1893, and his nephew Stanley Field directed it for three decades during its initial important growth period. The Oriental Institute was established in 1894 at the University of Chicago with Rockefeller funds. The Adler Planetarium was built in 1930 by the Max Adler family. The Museum of Science and Industry came about in 1926, thanks to the foresight and generosity of Julius Rosenwald, owner of Sears, Roebuck and Co. The important DuSable Museum of African-American History, one of the first in the country, opened in 1961 through the leadership of black citizens. The Museum of Contemporary Art followed in 1967 and moved into a much larger new building of startling design in 1996. The Terra Museum of American Art was built by Dan Terra in 1979 to house his outstanding collection. All were established through individual initiatives with private funds.

Moving west to California, our largest state in terms of population, even though it entered the Union later than the eastern states, we will see that the lessons and techniques developed by earlier museums were followed and enhanced. Edwin Bryant Crocker, a railroad attorney who lived in the state capital of Sacramento, was taken with art collecting, particularly works from California artists, when he retired. Adjacent to their home, the Crockers built a gallery to exhibit their art. Upon Judge Crocker's death, his widow bestowed the residence and their collection, consisting of more than seven hundred paintings and a thousand drawings, to the city of Sacramento. The year was 1884, which makes the Crocker Art Museum the first public museum in California, as well as the first museum in the west.

Michael Harry de Young, publisher of the *San Francisco Chronicle* newspaper, created the M. H. de Young Memorial Museum in 1894 to become the premier repository of American paintings in California. He did it by moving from Chicago to San Francisco the Egyptian Revival building which had been constructed for the 1893 World's Fair. The museum was so successful and became so overburdened with contributions of art that he built a larger building, which still stands.

Alma de Bretteville Spreckels, married to the sugar king Adolph Spreckels, was devoted to things French. Her collection consisted of paintings, furniture, tapestries and decorative arts, particularly from the seventeenth and eighteenth centuries. She brought about the building of a museum in San Francisco suitable to exhibit such art and named it The California Palace of the Legion of Honor. This was in 1924.

These two premier museums, which for years felt they were competitors, were united in 1972 under the banner of the Fine Art Museums of San Francisco. Nothing could be more appropriate.

Avery Brundage, an engineer and president of the International Olympic Committee for two decades, amassed a vast collection of Asian art. It included ceramics, bronzes, jade objects, paintings, lacquers and sculpture. He gave it all to the city of San Francisco to be housed in a new building built in 1969. Thus was the Asian Art Museum of San Francisco created.

In 1937, a group of collectors in Santa Barbara eyed the old Post Office building, which had stood empty for some time, and approached the city fathers with a proposition of leasing the building. The group then raised the funds to renovate the old building, donated their collections and paid for staffing and operation. The idea was accepted and in 1941 the new museum opened. Fifty-six years later the Santa Barbara Museum of Art has expanded four times, made possible by contributions of private funds exceeding $20 million; has permanent collections in excess of fifteen thousand objects; has established a $50 million endowment and has completed its latest addition of a new wing. Never has the city, county nor state been called upon to provide any funds. The principal collectors who made this possible are Wright Ludington, the Preston Morton family, Alice Keck Park, Jean & Austin Peck, Paul and Leslie Ridley-Tree, Carol Valentine, F. Bailey Vanderhoef, Jr., Zola & John Rex, Leigh Block and Mrs. Stanley McCormick—all amateurs.

There was a valuable by-product of the founding of the Santa Barbara Museum of Art. The Santa Barbara Art Association held its first exhibition in 1952. The University of California at Santa Barbara established a fine arts department about the same time.

The Los Angeles County Museum of Art, established in 1913 as a government department, had received token support as its collection grew slowly. Because of this heritage of being overly dependent on government funds, the museum has had a rather troubled history. In 1945 William Randolph Hearst made a large donation, which lifted the museum up a level or two. In 1965 the museum received its second private boost, when trustees raised $12 million to build a separate museum building and contributed works of art. Under this momentum the Ahmanson Gallery, Francis & Armand Hammer Wing, Leo S. Bing Center and Robert O. Anderson building were built and the Alice & Nasli Heeramaneck collection was received. Once again the amateurs had triumphed.

Marcia Weisman campaigned for years for a truly representative museum of contemporary art in Los Angeles. Eli Broad and Max Palevsky, both businessmen in the city, joined with her and raised the necessary funds for construction, additional millions for endowment and gave art as well.

Norton Simon, a food manufacturer and prolific art collector, initially became involved with the Los Angeles County Museum of Art, serving on its board and helping to make it a major museum. In all, Simon acquired over $100 million in art. He purchased, among other things, the Duveen Brothers Gallery in New York (Lord Joseph Duveen's company before his death) in its entirety, including 146 Old Masters paintings and much sculpture and rare books. Simon resigned from the Los Angeles County Museum's board over a dispute and eventually acquired the Pasadena Art Institute after it came upon troubled financial times, contributed his magnificent collection and renamed it the Norton Simon Museum. Upon his death, his wife took over the management of the museum and the foundation. It is a gem.

The Huntington Library, Art Gallery and Botanical Gardens is a classic accomplishment. Henry E. Huntington worked at real estate and transportation and as a pastime began collecting rare books. The more he learned, the more he acquired. By the time he had built his library on his estate in San Marino he had a vast collection of books and manuscripts, including more than five thousand incunabula, books published before 1501. It is one of the great research libraries in the world. Later, under the influence of his new wife, he became interested in art and assembled a handsome collection including twelve thousand British drawings and watercolors. This is a marvelous complex including gardens on two hundred acres. Don't miss it.

The story of the J. Paul Getty museum complex is nearly unbelievable. As the art author William Wilson stated, "The hobby of an amateur became the world's best endowed museum." J. Paul Getty spent his lifetime seeking and selling oil and did spectacularly well. When he found time from this demanding responsibility, he sought relaxation and enjoyment in collecting art and cultural objects. He started slowly, learning as he went. In a few years, his hobby became a passion, and he pursued the best the world had to offer. As his collection grew, he opened a modest museum in Malibu, California, for the public. When he died in 1976, the bulk of his fortune went to the trust that controlled the museum. Overnight it became the largest endowment of any museum in the world. Under the direction of Harold Williams, president and chief executive officer, the Getty has become one of the largest art complexes in the world, containing not only a museum but special institutes serving conservation, art education, research and grants. Nothing like it has ever been attempted. Frequently lost in the wonderment of this remarkable happening is the fact that all of the funds are private and they came from an amateur collector.

The first museum in California was founded in 1886. Over one hundred years later, the *Official Museum Directory*, published by the American Association of Museums, lists 495 museums now operating in California. There can be only a few communities who have not yet founded their own. The majority are privately supported and managed by private boards of trustees. The amateur collectors are the primary stimulus for the creation of these institutions. The idea of private support and control, established in the very first instance in America, has served California well.

Virtually all America's museums were started by citizens, not the government, constructed with private funds and organized as "not for profit" organizations. Many institutions charge modest admission fees a few days of the week to help pay for operating costs; other days are free so that everyone may visit. In contrast, the British National Gallery, founded and supported by Parliament, started charging admission in the 1920s to limit the attendance. They did not want visitors to disturb the artists who were copying pictures in the galleries! Of late, due largely to Director Neil MacGregor, admission is once again free.

The people liked their new institutions. Leaders of their communities responded by opening new museums, expanding those already established and pursuing the finest art, historical, scientific and educational materials in the world, wherever they were.

Between the two World Wars more than three hundred new museums were founded. Today the official guide lists three thousand museums; in 1996 alone, more than one hundred new museums were founded. Including historic sites and history museums raises the total count to eight thousand. When the Bicentennial was celebrated in 1976, forty Washington, D.C., museums participated. A hundred years earlier there were only two museums in our nation's capital. The value of the objects they own is in the billions of dollars. No accurate estimate exists because museums do not equate their holdings with dollars. Ninety percent of all objects housed in our institutions came to them as gifts. The balance were purchased by funds provided by private parties. Annual museum attendance is over 565 million, compared to a total of 118 million fans who attended all the major professional hockey, basketball, football and baseball games in

America in 1996. Another 130 million people annually attend museum programs held outside the museums' walls. Museum memberships are in the millions. People love their museums so much that the flow of gifts increases every year both in dollars and gifts of objects. Today practically every average-sized community has a museum of some description. Collectors have made them possible. They are as much a part of our cities and villages as are theaters and sport stadiums.

The people are so generous that forty percent of the museums today are planning additions in the next five years. In Seattle, for example, three major art museums have added a total of 200,000 square feet of space over the past five years—more than $4\frac{1}{2}$ acres! The largest, the Seattle Art Museum, has tripled in size and has added 2,550 pieces of art and 8,000 new members since 1991. The magnitude of our country's investment in saving, collecting, housing, exhibiting, conserving and restoring our nation's and the world's treasures is difficult to comprehend, it is so huge. We outspend the rest of the world combined. The conservation, preservation and exhibiting of fine cultural, educational, scientific and art objects is a booming activity.

Even today, only the largest of the museums have sufficient funds to acquire a major work. That money comes from private donations and/or from the sale of works that the museum decides it no longer needs for any one of many reasons. These objects usually are first offered to other museums. Should there be no interest, the works are then made available to the public through auction houses. The funds received from the sales are then used to acquire other objects. Because of the lack of large sums available for the purchase of art, our museums are still very dependent on gifts from collectors to enhance their collections.

The federal government has also been the beneficiary of loyal and generous collectors. J. Carter Brown, a former director of the National Gallery of Art, observed, "The United States does not have, as some nations do, a large pool of government owned art for the purpose of having American art on our embassies' walls." Consequently, an organization of private citizens set out some thirty years ago to ask for contributions and loans of art for this purpose from private collectors, museums, foundations, artists, galleries and corporations. No government funds were employed. At its last report, more than three thousand works of art had been donated or loaned for placement in 133 embassy posts in 116 countries. The group also raised funds for the conservation of this art. James A. Baker III, then Secretary of State, made this statement of thanks to the private collectors: "Your efforts to help other people understand the diversity, the depth and the quality of American culture have made the Department of State's mission more enjoyable and effective. I sincerely thank you for your very special gift to the nation." Similar activities have led to enhancing the State Department reception areas and the White House.

Lest we conclude that these precedent-setting efforts were solely a provincial drive to bring the world's treasures to America, we should be reminded of the stunning generosity of John D. Rockefeller, Jr. He paid for the restoration of Versailles, Fontainebleau and the Cathedral of Rheims when neither the French government nor the Catholic Church could or would provide the necessary funds. And as recently as 1997, the University of Chicago performed a rare on-site restoration in Egypt. After being faceless for fifteen hundred years, a statue of the ancient Egyptian goddess Mut was restored, thanks to a discovery by the University. The statue is now intact at the Colonnade Hall of Luxor Temple in Egypt. The Getty Museum, created by J. Paul Getty and his vast oil fortune, has become a new and unequaled force in support of conservation of the world's cultural treasures. They contribute money, staff and ideas to many countries. Under the direction of Harold Williams, the Getty organization has traveled new roads in philanthropy. They are doing things that were never done before—for example, providing millions of dollars each year for conservation, education and research grants, training of museum professionals and an art history program to help protect cultural objects through international agreements—on a scale that was unimaginable a decade ago. All of this is being accomplished with private funds. There are many other cases of American generosity preserving historically significant objects and sites around the world.

As a result of these extraordinary generous contributions by collectors, our museums now represent a huge body of knowledge and expertise. This is the reason so many colleges and universities now operate and maintain museums on their campuses. Alumni collectors have given their alma maters the wherewithal to build the structures and the collections to fill them. These institutions are now in a position to assist the present day collectors by providing information and encouragement.

Our museums have many essential responsibilities that make them important to our communities, to our cultural history and to the generations still to come. They collect, conserve, preserve, exhibit, entertain, market products through catalogues and some through their own stores, construct buildings like palaces and cathedrals and instill pride within their communities. Their ability to attract exhibitions of works from around the world is unequalled. The Metropolitan Museum of Art, for example, organized an exhibition called "The Glory of Byzantium," which consisted of 350 objects from twenty-four countries. It took the museum four years to arrange and stage such a complex exhibition. For hundreds of thousands of visitors, there was no other way for them ever to see these precious pieces. This is just one example of an extraordinary amount of time, money and talent expended to serve the public.

One role of the museum is that of a tastemaker. Exhibitions staged by museums help determine what we like and want and value. Having a piece featured in a museum catalogue adds to its value and appreciation. Objects that museums buy and sell determine market values and acceptance. When museums buy from dealers and auction houses, they add to their luster and credibility. As an object moves from private hands to a museum, several things happen. It now belongs to the people. There is much less chance of loss or damage. Many more people can view and appreciate it. It will be seen in a most handsome setting. It becomes a source of pride to the community, the staff and other artists.

In the history of the world, nothing has ever approached the American museum as a collecting agency. Its ability to collect objects is prodigious. No other society—not the Greeks nor the Romans nor the English at their peaks—even came close, particularly when the short period of time that America's museums have existed is considered. That is why we have so many museums serving the public and why we are still building new ones and expanding those that exist. The objects keep pouring in from generous collectors. The National President of the American Association of Museums stated publicly some time ago that acquisitions were a top priority and responsibility of museums. The American collector agrees and complies.

A revealing confirmation of the all-important role of private collectors to the conservation and preservation of our nation's most valued cultural, historic and artistic treasures was disclosed in a most unusual publishing event by *Time* magazine in 1997. An entire issue featured a beautifully illustrated, magnificent essay by Robert Hughes, the critic and author, entitled "American Visions—What America's Greatest Art Reveals about Our National Character." In all, fifty-one American artists and their creations are featured. Two of the works of art are in private hands. The remaining forty-nine are in public institutions as a result of gifts by collectors or purchases by private funds.

Joseph Alsop, the distinguished Washington correspondent, columnist and author, outlined the system that supports collecting (while it emphasizes art, the basics apply to all fields of collecting). Alsop describes the process as follows: "Art collecting is the basic by-product of art because the rest of the system would never have developed without art collecting. Nothing else will follow in the absence of the collector." Where the collector is present, museums, art history and the art market come into being. Once museums are established, art history as a major interest emerges. Indeed, this became a new academic study as recently as the 1920s, when Paul Sachs left his family investment banking business and joined Harvard's faculty to establish the first recognized degree-granting program in what may be called the study of connoisseurship. Many of our museum's leading directors came from Sachs's program.

As collectors became more active and increased in number, the market blossomed. Auction houses grew to serve the collector. Dealers expanded to assist the collector. Museums followed as collectors decided to give all or portions of their collections to the public. The flow of objects grew so rapidly that virtually every museum found it necessary to expand to accommodate the gifts. Hundreds of new museums were founded in communities that had never before had one.

The organizations that serve museums were all founded in the twentieth century: the American Association of Museums in 1906, the Association of Art Museum Directors in 1916 and the National Institute for the Conservation of Cultural Property in 1973 (now known as Heritage Preservation). Under the direction of president and chief executive officer Lawrence L. Reger and chairman Ross Merrill, this organization has been restoring to their original glory thousands of outdoor sculptures that had deteriorated badly under the attack of the elements. The American Institute for Conservation of Historic and Artistic Works, founded in 1972, is the research arm of the conservation field. It regularly publishes learned journals on the new findings and techniques to be used for the conservation of all objects of cultural, historic and artistic value.

With the rapidly growing interest in collecting by Americans and the increasing number of museums that private citizens were founding, it was only natural—perhaps inevitable—that the federal government would begin to participate. This it did by creating the National Endowment for the Arts and the

National Institute for the Humanities in 1965. Encouraged by their initial acceptance and performances, Congress established the Institute for Museum Services in 1976, now called the Institute for Museum and Library Services. Each is chartered to perform special and specific services for the arts, humanities and museums.

Attitudes toward collecting have changed, of course. At the turn of the century, the motivation was to introduce the general public to art and culture for the betterment of society. As our society was young and being formed, collecting added to one's social and economic prestige. Objects were purchased to decorate grand houses and mansions. Now a new attitude is making itself felt. Thanks to the educational programs fostered by museums, schools, universities, exhibitions, travel, dealers, auctions and a better educated populace, the attraction of collecting includes other appreciations as well. Young people are more flexible, open and daring. Collecting in some ways has become an "intriguing sport." Even when collectors sell their collections rather than giving them away, their names continue to draw interest and gain value. This is due to the fact that fine collections live on even when sold, owing to the importance of provenance—the history of the ownership of the pieces, which is often critical in appraising and valuing the object. Your collection after disposal carries your name in the provenance as a previous owner.

We have seen the tremendous dynamics of collecting and the distinctive role the American collector plays in our society and culture. As a collector, you join the ranks of some of the most remarkable people in our history, many of whom have made extraordinary contributions to our way of life and preserving and enriching our history.

Chapter 3

THE POWER OF AN IDEA – HOW A BANKER, A MERCHANT, A STOCKBROKER, A TEACHER AND A BUTCHER CHANGED THE MUSEUM WORLD

> *"All of these pictures are so valuable and so rare that they must be kept for the public, and a Gallery built for them. It is a fine thing to do for the nation and it is a fine thing for the family name also."*
>
> – Andrew Mellon

IT DID NOT HAPPEN OVERNIGHT. The idea was first expressed, somewhat wistfully, about 1922. It took fourteen years for it to be articulated formally and for an executive decision to be made that would allow its implementation, then another five years to reach completion of the first phase.

The man with the idea was Andrew Mellon. His first expression of it took place in Pittsburgh, Pennsylvania, where he had been born, lived and worked. A disturbingly quiet man, slight and sallow in appearance, cautious, conservative, secretive, slow to act and never before being absolutely sure—people rarely knew his true reaction—Mellon controlled the Mellon Bank, the Aluminum Company of America, the Koppers Company, Carborundum Company, the Gulf Oil Company and a mammoth fortune. His single marriage was a failure that ended in divorce when his wife left him for another man. (Despite his wife's flagrant behavior even while married to Mellon, he continued to care for her financially throughout her life and offered to remarry her when her lover-husband finally left her, but she refused.) The unhappiness of his marriage may have stimulated his interest in art, which grew every year. In his spare time, when not running his industrial and banking empire and during the final years of his marriage, Mellon began collecting art. He visited Europe every year. Every year he returned to his home in Pittsburgh with another batch of masterpieces, for he was interested only in the very best.

As Mellon viewed his growing collection, the idea came to him—America should have its own National Gallery of Art. It should be located in the nation's capital. It should house only the finest art the world had to offer. Even as he continued with his burdensome business activities and then added to them, at the request of three presidents of the United States, the responsibility of serving as Secretary of the Treasury for over ten years, the idea never left him. Each year he edged closer to the realization of his magnificent dream. He acquired art at an accelerating pace as though he knew he had only a little time left. His taste for the treasures of the world never died. In the early 1930s, in the depth of the Depression, the Russian government, searching for hard cash, sold of some of its priceless art from the Hermitage. For $6,654,000, Mellon was able to acquire twenty-one paintings, including Botticelli's *Adoration of the Magi* and Titian's *Venus with a Mirror* as well as works by Raphael, Rembrandt and Hals. If it weren't for Mellon, these masterpieces would not be in our National Gallery today. His final purchase of art in 1934 through Lord Joseph Duveen, the international art dealer, was the largest ever recorded at that time. He established foundations to provide long-range financial support for his idea. He researched other museums to determine what did and did not work. He had Washington, D.C., surveyed for the best possible location, including areas for future expansion. He employed architects and art experts and recruited senior staff. It was probably the most thorough and disciplined program ever developed in the museum field at the time. He approached this project exactly as he had faced dozens of other enterprises in creating his industrial empire. Nothing was left to chance. Now he was finally ready.

In 1936, he wrote President Franklin D. Roosevelt offering to build at his own expense a National Gallery of Art. He would provide an endowment and give his entire art collection to the people of America to be housed in the new National Gallery. There were no strings. Indeed, one of the most remarkable parts of his offer to the nation was that it would be known as the National Gallery and his name would not appear on the building. President Roosevelt called this one of most selfless acts he had ever witnessed and accepted Mellon's offer immediately, as did Congress. Mellon's gift of art, the building and endowment was the largest ever made to a government anywhere by anyone. Thus was born our nation's National Gallery of Art.

Construction was started soon after, and the gallery was completed and opened in 1941, the year of Pearl Harbor. Sadly, Andrew Mellon had died in 1937; he never saw the completion of his grand idea nor was he able to see his world-class art collection exhibited in the new building.

Mellon's proposal that his name not be identified with the National Gallery was not just an altruistic act, despite President Roosevelt's proclamation. It was a practical strategy. Mellon knew, great as his own collection was, it was not sufficient to carry a National Gallery into the forefront of museums worldwide by itself. Other collectors had to be encouraged to do the same if the National Gallery was to fulfill Mellon's dream, and he knew this would be very difficult, if not impossible, if the gallery were named the Andrew Mellon Museum of Art. Also a national gallery, virtually by definition, could not be named for an individual. There could only ever be one National Gallery of Art.

Nevertheless, this could not have been an easy or automatic decision by Mellon. There was precedent for naming major gifts given to the people through the federal government for the people who made the gifts. When James Smithson, an Englishman, left 100,000 British pounds (then a huge sum) to the United States "to found in Washington, under the name of the Smithsonian Institution, an establishment for the increase and diffusion of knowledge among men," Congress accepted the gift and its terms, naming the museum the Smithsonian Institution. Smithson is buried in the original building. The year was 1846. Today the Smithsonian is the largest museum-research complex in the world. From its rather hesitant beginning—Congress debated for some time whether it would accept the gift—the Smithsonian now consists of several separate units including the National Zoological Park, Astrophysical Observatory, Museum of Natural History, Freer Gallery of Art, National Museum of American History, National Museum of American Art, National Portrait Gallery, Hirshhorn Museum and Sculpture Garden, National Air & Space Museum, the Sackler Gallery and the Cooper-Hewitt Museum. (The reader has undoubtedly noted that several of the units of the Smithsonian are named for individuals.) Indeed, for federal government bureaucratic reasons, the National Gallery of Art is listed in small type as being a bureau of the Smithsonian, although its management is outside the province of the Smithsonian and governed by a board composed of a majority of independent directors. Also, the gallery has its own endowment and receives operating funds directly from Congress, which enables it to offer free admission at all times. This has been a happy and productive private-public partnership under which the National Gallery has flourished.

We now enter the second phase of the development of the National Gallery. Could the new National Gallery attract other donors and thus become a truly world-class museum of art?

The answer was a resounding "Yes." In the time frame of the museum world, the response was almost immediate. Four other collectors, one after the other, joined with Andrew Mellon in contributing their outstanding collections to the people through the newly established National Gallery. Each had reasons to give their collections to other institutions and all were constantly being entreated to do so. Yet in the end they found the idea that Andrew Mellon had sparked and developed more powerful than any and all other inducements.

The first was Samuel H. Kress. Born in Pennsylvania, he began his career as a schoolteacher. From his rather meager savings, he then bought a small novelty store; following its success under his management, he opened a second store. That, too, succeeded and Kress was off. He built a chain of 5 & 10 cent stores and made a fortune. He started traveling on vacations to Europe, where he was introduced to art. At first he turned to buying art to ward off boredom. Then, like so many, he became addicted and started buying art in earnest.

Several museums took an interest in Kress's collection. Upon Andrew Mellon's death, Kress became art dealer Joseph Duveen's largest client. Duveen, who had helped Mellon assemble his collection for the National Gallery, encouraged Kress to consider the same. The persuasive director of the National Gallery, David Finley, whom Mellon had installed, made frequent visits to Kress. When John Walker succeeded Finley as director he continued the courtship. Kress became impressed with Walker, in part because of Walker's long and close association with Bernard Berenson, the expatriate art historian and scholar who had assisted Kress with some of his acquisitions.

Eventually the National Gallery received the choicest selections of Kress's magnificent collection. The initial gift consisted of 393 paintings and sculptures. In appreciation, Kress was named president of the gallery. Shortly thereafter, he was crippled by a massive stroke and never left his bed. The board of the National Gallery voted to have him continue as president. Walker paid him visits in his New York home, frequently as often as once a week. Kress's brother Rush took over management of his foundation and continued to buy outstanding works of art, which were also assigned to the gallery—$25 million worth in the years from 1946 to 1956. A complete cataloguing of the Samuel H. Kress collection was published in nine volumes. Many museums were recipients of works from the Kress collection, although the National Gallery received the finest. Thus the idea of the National Gallery had been endorsed by one of the most prolific collectors of all time.

Another Pennsylvanian, Joseph Widener, born and raised in Philadelphia, also made a significant impact on the National Gallery. Widener's father, Peter A. B. Widener, had been a butcher in Philadelphia and made his fortune providing the Union Army with meat during the Civil War. He then entered the local transit business after the war and made another fortune. With this he acquired a collection largely composed of Old Masters paintings, statuary and decorative arts. He built a mansion on the Main Line to house his collection. Upon his death in 1915, he passed control of the collection to his son Joseph.

Over the years, the son pursued several avenues for the eventual disposition of his father's collection, which at the time was considered the finest in private hands. He had a few special requirements regarding how the works should be exhibited, to which the National Gallery finally agreed. In 1942 the entire collection was given to the National Gallery. Unfortunately, Joseph died shortly before the collection was installed in the new gallery. Very probably, if the National Gallery had not been founded when it was, this magnificent collection would now be residing in a Philadelphia museum.

But the story is not yet over.

Lessing Rosenwald, son of Julius, who controlled Sears, Roebuck & Co., was born in Chicago to wealth and position and continued the family's participation in Sears. He also began to collect a wide variety of things including books, woodcuts, etchings, engravings, lithographs—more than 22,000 works in all. During World War II, while serving in Washington, D.C., he became familiar with the new National Gallery of Art and with David Finley, the director. Rosenwald gave his entire art collection to the National Gallery in 1943.

The last of the five collectors who made the National Gallery of Art the prestigious institution it has become was Chester Dale. Born and raised in New York, he was as different from the others as one could be. A rough, tough stockbroker and bond dealer, he made his fortune on Wall Street and became a most astute buyer of art. He and his wife acquired such a volume of art that he was forced to loan much of it to several museums. He had portraits of himself painted by many artists including George Bellows, Diego Rivera and Dali. Dale loved a good martini as much as some of his art, and he and his wife lived grandly—at either his penthouse at the Carlyle Hotel or the Plaza Hotel while in New York, summers on Long Island and winters in Palm Beach. The board of the National Gallery, anxious to garner at least a portion of his collection, named him president, a position he held for ten years. John Walker was available to visit Dale every week or as often as necessary. Paul Mellon, son of Andrew Mellon and most active as a board member, also met with Dale as required. Upon his death in 1962, the collection went to the National Gallery. It consisted of 252 paintings and sculptures, including works of Toulouse-Lautrec, Modigliani, Monet, Picasso and Van Gogh. He had paid about $2 million to acquire his collection; it was valued at $50 million when he bequeathed it to the Gallery and it is worth many times that figure today. Dale left some fine paintings to the Metropolitan Museum of Art as well.

Following the example of the "Magnificent Five," scores of individuals started making contributions of art to the National Gallery—so much so that within a decade, the National Gallery was considered one of the world's great museums—a remarkable feat never duplicated in so short of period. Even Andrew Mellon, on his most optimistic day, could not have envisioned such acceptance.

Finley and Walker played critical roles in acquiring these magnificent collections for the National Gallery to follow Andrew Mellon's initial gift. In fact, a vital part of this success story is due to the remarkable men who served as its directors. Over the first fifty-five years only four have been called to direct the affairs of the gallery. The first, David Finley, was appointed by Andrew Mellon and was key in the design and building of the gallery as well as successfully encouraging other collectors to give to the gallery. John Walker succeeded Finley and continued the winning process of obtaining contributions of works of art from collectors. As he once observed, "The greater part of my adult life has been spent collecting collectors who would, I hoped, become donors. That was my principal job as museum curator and later as a museum director, positions I held for over 30 years." J. Carter Brown followed Walker and served the longest. He oversaw and directed the design and building of the marvelous new wing needed to contain the flood of art treasures given to the gallery by appreciative collectors. Earl A. Powell III, who had been executive curator of the National Gallery before leaving to become director of the Los Angeles County Museum of Art, returned as director with the retirement of Brown. He knows the gallery well and had a most distinguished tour as director of the Los Angeles museum for over a decade.

Other museums which have benefited from the skills and experince of long-term directors are the Metropolitan, where director Phillippe de Montebello has served with great distinction for twenty years, and the Art Institute of Chicago, where James N. Wood has presided for nearly two decades and led the museum through its greatest period of growth. His unerring eye was responsible for making the museum once again one of the most handsome and glorious in the world as every exhibition area was redone and new wing added. Ann d'Haroncourt, one of the growing number of women being recognized in the museum field, has had a brilliant career as director of the Philadelphia Museum of Art. She follows in the path established by Fiske Kimball, first director of the museum and responsible for gaining many impressive collections. Katherine Lee, after several years as assistant director of the Art Institute of Chicago, was named director of the Virginia Museum of Art, leading that institution to new levels of community participation. John Walsh, director of the Getty Museum of Art, has overseen the largest building program in the museum field during the twentieth century, while at the same time continuing the Getty's program of acquiring preeminent art. Edward Pillsbury, with one of the most distinguished of academic credentials, as director of the Kimball Museum in Fort Worth, Texas, has made it a major force in the museum field. Dr. William Boyd led the Field Museum of Natural History to new levels of research prominence. Harry S. Parker, director of the Fine Arts Museums of San Francisco, guided the museum during its trying period of restoration and seismic upgrading. Ellsworth Brown brought financial strength while expanding the Chicago Historical Society. Sherman Lee, the legendary director of the Cleveland Museum, practiced disciplines that established standards in the field. He followed William Milliken's forty years of service. Two of the twentieth century's most accomplished directors, Francis Henry Taylor of the Metropolitan and Daniel Catton Rich of the Art Institute of Chicago, closed their careers at the Worcester Art Museum in Massachusetts. Richard E. Oldenburg, director of the Museum of Modern Art in New York City, guided the expansion of the museum's building and collections and recruited and designed outstanding exhibitions during his long tenure. Otto Wittmann has had a remarkable career: After leading the Toledo Museum to national recognition and then retiring, the Los Angles County Museum of Art asked Otto to serve as advisor and trustee. When that task was completed, the Getty Museum asked him to do the same and elected him Vice-Chairman.

Certainly S. Dillon Ripley, Secretary of the Smithsonian Institution, has to be proclaimed one the most imaginative and productive. During the twenty years of his leadership the

Smithsonian added eight new museums and established the *Smithsonian* magazine, which became a tremendous success and a substantial contributor to the financial well-being of the institution. Paul Perrot, director of the Corning Museum for several years before joining Dillon Ripley at the Smithsonian, went on to the Virginia Museum of Fine Arts for a near decade and then to the Santa Barbara Museum of Art before retiring. He is recognized as one of the most knowledgeable and articulate experts in the area of conservation.

There are many other distinguished directors. These few serve only as examples of the quality and skills all museums should search for. As the number of museums grows and others expand, the demand for professional competence in managing our invaluable institutions increases, for a museum's value to its community can be magnified many times with the employment of top-flight staffs, led by the director.

Still, the most remarkable part of this fascinating, almost unbelievable tale, is that the National Gallery of Art was created and bequeathed to all of us by five amateurs—a banker, a merchant, a stockbroker, a teacher and a butcher. It could only happen in America.

Chapter 4

WHY PEOPLE COLLECT – SECRETS OF THE GREAT COLLECTORS

"A man must leave some sort of track."
– Thomas Gilcrease, founder of the Gilcrease Institute of American History and Art

"Men may come and men may go, but books go on forever. The ownership of a fine library is the surest and swiftest way to immortality."
– Henry E. Huntington, founder of the Huntington Library

"Why do men and women collect? As well ask why they fall in love. The reasons are irrational."
– Kenneth Clark, former director of the National Gallery, London

ACCORDING TO THE MEMOIRS of Lomenie de Brieme, assistant to the great Cardinal Mazarin, the aged and dying cardinal shuffled slowly through his galleries in his nightshirt and slippers, viewing his great art collection perhaps for the last time. He exclaimed over and over, "I must leave them all. How much time and care I have taken to collect my treasures and now I must say farewell. Now I must leave them all." Many collectors come to feel this way.

The cardinal's words and the quotations above, from dedicated collectors who left the bulk of their treasures to the people, capture the intensity, passion and dedication that can develop as one enters this noble field of human activity. There are multiple motivations that move and direct collectors. Many collectors obviously follow more than one. But whatever persuades and drives an individual as a collector, the result is universally one that brings joy and satisfaction to a degree that is rarely equaled.

In fact, the sheer pleasure of collecting is one of the primary reasons people engage in the activity. A noted collector put it this way: "We are a happy group of people who collect for the joy and excitement of it." J. Paul Getty agrees: "Few human activities provide greater personal gratification than assembling a collection. Excitement, romance, drama and sense of accomplishment and triumph are all present in collecting." According to Paul Mellon, collecting stems from "a desire to own, to enjoy, to savor and to conserve rare and beautiful things, a desire which must infuse all collectors. The feeling begins in childhood. It is the childish pleasure of searching for rare and beautiful shells on the beach with the unclouded vision of the child." Even Bernard Berenson, the world-renowned art critic and historian, claimed of his collection: "The gathering of these books is the only thing I have accomplished in my life which gives me real satisfaction."

Many collectors find the hunt itself to be exciting. Lew Manilow, a contemporary art collector, asks and answers the question, "Why do I collect? I get emotionally and intellectually involved. I look for the quickening of the blood, a pounding of the heart and a fascination for reasons I cannot explain." There is a special thrill and a sense of contributing when you are responsible for uncovering or rediscovering a valuable object presumed lost. Pioneering, doing something for the first time or being one of the first to do so, can be especially rewarding. There is also the thrill of the purchase. Collectors testify to the excitement of winning a bidding battle at auction or of finding an important missing link in their collection. It equals any athletic or business victory. David Karpeles, manuscript collector, confesses, "Finding a great document is better than cotton candy, watermelon and sex."

Simply looking at the artworks or objects they have collected provides joy to all real collectors. The eye has a rapacious appetite and nothing substitutes for the viewing of beautiful things. All of us want exquisite things around us and what better way to placate this need than to collect objects of loveliness and meaning. Every area we occupy requires things of beauty and importance to us, and often collections are used to decorate our home and/or place of work.

Another reason people collect is for posterity: they wish to preserve either their own name and fame or the actual objects in their collection over time. "Every man wants to connect his life with something he thinks eternal," said Andrew Mellon. Few accomplishments receive as universal acclaim as the creation of a fine collection. The idea of glory never dies. "J. Paul Getty wanted to make sure his name was perpetuated as long as there was a civilization," according to Norris Branlett, Getty's personal aide, director and trustee of the Getty Museum. The fear of being forgotten caused the Egyptian Pharaohs to spend much of their lives building their own Mausoleums. The Pharaoh Tutankhamen insisted that his collection of canes be buried with him. "When the rulers of kingdoms today have crumbled into dust and their names forgotten of the people, the memory of a maker of a great collection will be a household word in the mouths of thousands. This is the real road to fame," according to George D. Smith, a noted collector and dealer.

Often times collections benefit posterity by preserving or adding to our cultural heritage. Art is a form of retaining memories, images, concepts; without art, these would be lost for all time. Many works of art have been around for centuries. People sense a feeling of continuity and history through owning such pieces. An appetite for exquisite antiquity will not die.

Every reader of this book has been the beneficiary of collectors who preceded him or her and left collections that we now enjoy at will. Scholars and students have access to vitally important material that would not be available were it not for the private collector who gathered the material and then gave it to our country. "Our number-one reason is to preserve the condition of our materials," says Francis Rouse of the Huntington Library. "A rare book or manuscript is a fragile item. We try to slow down the deterioration process." Thomas Jefferson made an even more plaintive plea: "I cannot live without books. Time and accidents are committing daily havoc on original papers. Let us save what remains."

In fact, sharing one's knowledge and the pleasure one gets from this avocation is another motivation for collecting. "Give to the public so that they may serve future generations," says a chairman of a leading research library. "The zeal and knowledge of private collectors have made contributions of inestimable value to scholarship," says the president of the University of Minnesota.

When one collects things of value and interest, it is especially rewarding to share them with friends and family. Your family may and should become involved, which will add to their happiness and your own. A collection can also be educational: stamp collecting, for example, can be an interesting and potentially profitable way to teach your children and grandchildren history and geography.

So many collectors comment on the lasting influence of having been introduced to collecting by their parents, relatives or friends. Your activity may stimulate members of your family to follow suit and start collecting in support of your interest or on their own. It may be through the traditional hobbies of stamp and coin collecting or even marbles. Carter Burden, who assembled an extraordinary collection of American literature as an adult noted, "I started collecting toy soldiers and baseball cards when I was six years old. I've kept the toy soldiers all these years." Colleen Moore, an early motion picture star, was launched into a lifetime of collecting minatures by her father's gift to her of a minature dictionary as a child. Later she had built what many consider the most famous doll house in the world. Actually a castle, with a great hall chapel and King Arthur's dining room, it now sits in Chicago's Museum of Science and Industry, where it delights hundreds of thousands of children every year.

Whatever it is that adults use to introduce children to collecting, its rewards last a lifetime. Finally, your children may be your inheritors. In that instance, your collections take on added importance.

For some, collecting is less a conscious choice than an inbred acquisitive instinct. We all must collect something because that instinct is inherent in each of us. "Collecting seems to be a universal and instinctive avocation," said Henry Francis Taylor, a former director of the Metropolitan Museum of Art. Mankind has been a collector throughout history—weapons, seeds, art on cave walls. Collecting can be an emotional endeavor. It can be a way to self-expression through possessions. To many, collecting is primarily a means of expression. It has little or nothing to with things we must use. Oscar Wilde, author, observed "Art is the most intense mode of individualism." Collecting can enlarge our experience. There is no dead past. Collectors can bring life to almost everything. In doing so, we add to our own experience and enjoyment.

The collector is never alone psychologically. He or she can find deep emotional connections with the past through their dedication and passion. And in a more present sense, you meet new friends. In my own experience, through collecting, I have met people from all over the world who would never have crossed my path otherwise. Without exception, they have been very interesting and have contributed to my knowledge and well-being.

Financially speaking, collecting can be a good investment (see Chapter 15, "The Economics"). It can also offer a public relations benefit to companies for being collectors, conservators and contributors. Corporations do not contribute to cultural institutions out of charitable impulses alone. They realize the general public appreciates their efforts to support worthwhile public programs. On a personal level, collecting offers the prestige of ownership. Ownership of rare, beautiful and valuable objects bestows prestige on the owner because peers recognize the dedication and effort that has gone into acquiring and caring for such objects. As one collector half-facetiously observed, "Even insincere adulation is a kick."

The importance of fully understanding why you are collecting and the final results you hope to achieve is dramatized by this tale of two collectors from the same period who had totally different objectives although they were collecting the same material.

The time is the late nineteenth and early twentieth century. The scene is New York City, where the two lived within ten minutes of each other. They were both wealthy men, having inherited money and businesses which they ran. They were both determined to amass the finest library then in existence and pursued rare books and portfolios wherever they happened to be and whatever they cost. They died within three years of each other.

One ordered in his will that his magnificent collection be sold. He had spent fifty years building his library; it was so large, more than sixteen thousand rare books and manuscripts, that it took nineteen months and seven sales to complete its disbursement. His stately residence, which housed his library, has been demolished and a skyscraper office building occupies the site. His name was Robert Hoe III. He is now known only for the fact that he had his collection sold.

The other had made provisions to have his residence and attached library preserved along with his collection for use by scholars and to be open to the public. His name was J. P. Morgan.

His library is known as the Pierpont Morgan Library. Scholars from around the world visit and use it. The flow of rare materials to it continues and the library has been expanded with the public's assistance and gratitude. The Morgan name lives on, as does the service he provided.

Hoe believed that his collection should be disbursed so that others would have the joy of collecting rare objects as he did. Ironically, the bulk of his collection was purchased by other collectors, including Morgan, and now resides in Morgan's magnificent library as well as in the Huntington Library and other leading libraries in America.

A tale of two similar objectives, two different results.

Chapter 5

HOW TO START A COLLECTION – KEY STEPS TO COLLECTING WITHOUT HEARTACHE

"Almost anyone can become a collector—and can start at almost any period of his or her life. I think that much of the hesitancy of the would-be collector will vanish if he or she simply bears in mind that every collector was once a beginner."

– J. Paul Getty

"I had no idea what was going to happen. I just bought what I loved."

– Joseph Hirshhorn, donor of the Hirshhorn Museum and Sculpture Garden, Smithsonian Institution

THE FIRST STEP in starting a collection is to select an area of interest. This is one of the most individualistic of all choices. There are no standards or guidelines to point your way. One person may find the ultimate in a certain area while another deplores the same subject. You may notice this during a stroll through a museum. The appeal of various works of art varies immensely between groups of people; indeed, there may be as many variations on an interest level as there are people. Contemporary art serves as a dramatic example of our different tastes and interests. Some become avid collectors while to others this art is at best a complete mystery. Before you commit, allow yourself an extravagant period of considering many possibilities, including those with which you have no familiarity. You are apt to be surprised at how many ideas are unlocked and how arresting fresh concepts can become. The least this spirited exercise will reveal are a number of things you definitely do not wish to pursue. Even better, it may carry you to places and designs that can bring new enthusiasms and energy to your most creative program.

Have a sense of history. Review your family's background. Ask yourself what your children and grandchildren would like to have twenty to thirty years from now. Consider the big factors that influenced your life—your parents; a war; where you went to college; your work experience; travel; special studies; civic or charitable efforts; extraordinary people you may have met; where you have lived; happenings for which you are particularly grateful, such as a gift; an illness from which you dramatically recovered; or an unexpected surprise that brought you something beyond your hopes and dreams. Any one or all of these thoughts may launch you on an interesting, exciting collecting experience. Do not be tame. Release your imagination, challenge yourself to reach out. Enthuse. Be compulsive.

Upon completion of this interrogation of your own likes, dislikes and passions (perhaps hidden) you will have taken the decisive first step to becoming one of America's most deserving benefactors—a dedicated collector.

Now comes the time for discipline. Do as much reading as possible about the area you have selected. Become curious about every angle of your subject. Your local library will be of help. Visit museums and their exhibitions. They have massive resources. This will train your eye and make you more discerning. Identify the established dealers in your area of interest. Visit them to get a sense of prices and an understanding of their practices. Get on their mailing lists. Talk to other collectors to learn from them—

How to Start a Collection

they have already made most of the common mistakes. This will help you develop "street smarts." Associations, clubs and societies frequently exist for certain collecting areas, such as books, china, coins, stamps and so forth. Read their publications and subscribe. Perhaps there is a club or association you can join. Attend its conventions.

The next step is to actually begin collecting. First, research your own holdings—you may find you have a small start already underway without being aware of it. Determine where you want to keep your collection, or perhaps display it. Establish a record-keeping format. Computers can be of assistance, and fun when you learn how. Correspond with other collectors. Attend auctions and obtain their reports and catalogues. Rely on experts, museum directors and curators, established dealers, educators. You wouldn't buy stock from someone you don't know. Don't buy objects you are collecting that way either.

There are some areas in which you can start immediately and it is difficult to go wrong: objects you normally need for your home such as furniture, art for your walls and books. Antiques are fascinating. Books are intriguing. Art for your walls is a little more fraught with doubts from time to time, but you will need art anyway, so why not try to acquire objects of special interest to you—even works that are dazzling or fancy or arrestingly colorful. For example, although I have never been a compulsive collector of paintings and drawings, I have developed an interesting series for me—that is works of art done by persons I know who are primarily amateurs. They are surprisingly good and the fact that they were created by amateurs, not to mention acquaintances, adds much to our enjoyment of each piece—and to their conversation value!

If chosen well and carefully, these three categories appreciate in value every decade. The insurance companies will testify to that. In most cases your children will appreciate them as well when it is time for you to pass them on. Many have received valued pieces from parents and relations that grace their homes today.

49

There are many organizations, societies and associations whose purposes are to help collectors. Your local library and museums are good starting points to help you locate a group that provides information on collecting and collectibles. Chances are you will be able find one that specializes in the area of your interest.

There are several key "value" checkpoints you should employ as you start or build your collection. Each acquisition should be subjected to a number of critical probes.

The rarity of an object clearly dictates price. A book with an author's autograph is more valuable than an identical copy without the signature because the first is rarer. Similarly, an original painting is more desirable than a reproduction and a print from an edition limited to a small number is preferred to that from an unlimited large edition.

As soon as an object is created, it starts to deteriorate. Those objects that are well cared for, whose condition is superior, deserve and receive greater value. Suggestions for proper care of your collection are carried in Chapter 6.

Collectors live in a world full of fakes and frauds. Even the most experienced museums are sometimes fooled. One of the most valuable assets any object may have is unquestioned authenticity. Keys to determining this may be found in Chapter 14.

Prices may fluctuate widely and wildly. It is very easy to overpay. Careful investigation will save you both money and frustration. It can take decades to overcome the tendency to pay too high a price. See Chapters 11, 13, 14 and 15 to learn some of the keys to protecting yourself with regard to prices.

An established market makes it easier to determine proper value and to sell an object should you so desire. That's why many collectors buy through auction houses and dealers.

A collector's item is a piece of property, just as a house or automobile is. You would not think of acquiring either of the latter without a foolproof title; the same applies to objects you collect. Insist on proof of title before buying anything.

A carefully prepared and accurate record of previous ownership helps establish the object's authenticity. In addition, a distinguished provenance may add to the value of an object. Previous ownership by a famous or well-respected person can contribute a certain cachet that increases interest. Witness the astounding prices paid for Jaqueline Kennedy Onassis's items at auction. Most articles went for many times their estimates just because they had belonged to her.

Certain objects may have special historic interest that adds to their value. Items having been owned by presidents, heads of state or others in the political arena fit this category. Again this was seen in the Onassis auction, where President John Kennedy's belongings brought unbelievable prices, as well as in the auction of the gowns of Diana, Princess of Wales.

Chapter 6

THE CARDINAL RULES FOR COLLECTING – HOW TO BECOME A SUCCESSFUL COLLECTOR EVEN IF YOU ARE NOT RICH

"Collecting is a complex and irrepressible expression of the inner individual, a sort of devil, of which great personalities are frequently possessed."
– Francis Henry Taylor, early museum director

"Patience, discretion, integrity and just plain good business judgment are all necessary to acquire objects of more than average quality."
– Otto Wittmann, director emeritus of the Toledo Museum of Art

"Mr. Havemeyer has two great credentials for a collector. He has the flair and the nerve."
– Louisine Havemeyer, collector

COLLECTING, like every activity, has a few rules and traditions that will add immeasurably to the pleasure and success of any collector. Of course, each discipline will have its own standard practices, and each collector probably harbors his or her own special "do"s and "don't"s. A discussion of this nature will never be complete. In general, however, learning the rules will save money, time, and embarrassment. This includes educating yourself in the terminology used in your special area of interest.

The first, and perhaps most important "rule" is that quality comes first. Julian Ganz, a noted collector, once claimed that "The best buys we made were the objects we paid top price for." Or as Lord Joseph Duveen put it, "When you pay a high price for the priceless, you are getting it cheap." Of course, a high price tag alone does not make an object valuable. The successful collector must be able to determine an object's inherent value on his or her own.

To do this, you must develop your eye. The amateur collectors who built our museums developed sharp eyes for quality by carefully observing and studying objects. Once you have honed your eye, you should concentrate; be a collector, not an accumulator.

You need to become an expert in your area of interest. One thing you can do to educate yourself is build a library. If your area of collecting is the arts, you should spend time in artists' studios and get to know them. You should also read the critics. They may play favorites, but they are more knowledgeable than most and can be quite helpful. Another way to learn is to visit museums regularly and read their catalogues and journals. Discover what they are buying and selling. Museums are not only the taste makers, they help set the market. Mary Cassatt, the great American Impressionist and advisor to the Havemeyers as they put together their magnificent collection, prepared for acquisitions of Spanish paintings by visiting every major museum in Spain and by purchasing all the photographs available of El Greco's works. By thus preparing herself, she was better able to evaluate paintings and to separate the original works of art from any forgeries.

Even once you have become knowledgeable about your subject, you must remain vigilant. Don't rush into purchases without close attention. It would not hurt to follow Andrew

Mellon's practices. First, he relied on careful investigation. He obtained the opinions of others, then weighed the pros and cons in his own mind, taking ample time before making a decision. J. P. Morgan never purchased anything sight unseen, frequently insisting that the works be sent to him so that he could study them for a period of time before buying.

It will help to find a discerning and trusted advisor. Mrs. Potter Palmer and the Havemeyers benefited greatly from the advice of Mary Cassatt, who lived in Paris most of her life and became friendly with the French Impressionists. The paintings they acquired with her help increased immensely in value and many now hang in the most prestigious museums. Advisors will work with a collector on a commission or a fee basis. Their point of strength is that, unlike a dealer, they have nothing to sell except knowledge and service and so will be objective. But nothing is without risk. It is not unheard-of for an advisor to be sued by well-known collectors for fraud.

Know your people, whether they be advisors or sources. Dealers, auction houses, collecting groups, fairs, or sales may all be sources for you. Get to know them as they do you. Both Andrew Mellon and J. P. Morgan purchased most of their art through dealers whom they trusted: Mellon used Duveen and Knoedler, who operated as both a dealer and an advisor, and Morgan sought the advice of art dealer Seligmann. But neither of them blindly followed the advice they were given. *Caveat emptor* means you.

Financing your collection is another important issue. Follow auction prices, which are often a good indicator of the market. Using online services can sometimes save you money when buying art. An art collector was considering buying a Matisse drawing from a dealer. Using ArtNet, an online data base, he found that similar works had sold recently for 25 percent less than the dealer was asking. Doing his homework saved him more than $30,000 on his purchase. Decide on a "collecting budget." This can provide you with an important discipline (but don't be afraid to exceed your budget for special opportunities). It would be wise to start out slowly, with a few inexpensive objects. Do not "over invest" to begin with. J. Paul Getty started collecting Chinese and Japanese lacquer boxes on a trip to the Orient in 1912; his first purchases cost less than $100. Paul Sachs first bought color reproductions as a boy. If you are still unsure of yourself, consider collecting objects that can be purchased at auctions and from dealers. This indicates that a market exists.

Be passionate about your purchases, and don't buy primarily as a financial investment. "I have never bought pictures as an investment," claimed one of the world's most knowledgeable collectors, Paul Mellon. Business executive collector Eli Broad observes "Collecting is not just buying objects. It is really a learning experience you have to have a passion for." Add to your collection regularly and consistently. Keep everlastingly at it. J. Paul Getty said, "I am not only an addict when it comes to collecting, I am a chronic prevaricator when I determine I will stop collecting." John G. Johnson, a lawyer for Morgan and an avid collector, noted, "I swear off collecting weekly and swear on again semi-weekly."

Once you have established your collection, protect it. Learn how to care for your treasures. All objects start to deteriorate the moment they are created. The biographer of Kenneth Clark, retired director of the National Gallery in London, noted that his magnificent library of over 20,000 volumes, housed in a cold, dank and damp castle room, had deteriorated badly. Mildew, cracking and flaking of the leather bindings and an invasion of bookworms had severely damaged his books, many of them priceless. One would have thought he would have known better. "Time is a merciless editor," notes Ross Merrill, chief of conservation at the National Gallery of Art.

Even museums can fall prey to carelessness. A current event dramatizes the importance of caring for one's attention. Workers at a museum in The Hague dropped a rare and precious fossil while moving it from one location to another and it broke into 188 pieces.

There are simple steps you should take to protect your prizes from excessive wear, tear and damage from the elements. The American Institute for Conservation of Historic and Artistic Works in Washington, D.C., operates a nationwide referral system of conservators and a list of regional and local conservation organizations. They will put you in touch with experts who can help you. Another good source is the book *Caring for Your Collections* published by Harry N. Abrams, Inc.

Be adequately insured, which also means having an accurate appraisal. Before deciding on either an appraiser or insurance company, ask about their qualifications and expertise in your field of interest and obtain references. Ask to see examples of their work. Discuss their charges up front.

Keep complete records that include description of the object, when acquired, from whom and for how much, its condition, provenance, title, invoices, bill of sale, and any documents that refer to the object. Sterling Clark, founder with his wife, Francine, of the Sterling and Francine Clark Art Institue in Williamsburg, Massachusetts, kept diaries that covered his visits to dealers, museums, auction houses and other collectors. He used them to record market prices, conversations, pertinent correspondence and other information that was helpful to his collecting. It is very important that you keep photographs of each object as well. You will need them in case of losses and gifts you may make. They will also serve as research material. Store all these records separate from your collection in case of fire or other disaster.

Secure your collectibles from burglars and thieves. Security systems are desirable. Check out employees carefully. Observe simple procedures such as outside lighting, not making it noticeable that you are out of town and properly securing windows and doors. Your insurance company can be of help.

Have good legal counsel—for gifts, for sales, and for heirs. Plan to give at least a portion of your collection to your favorite institution. It will share your treasures with generations to come.

Above all, be careful, but don't be cynical—it can rob you of many joys.

None of these rules are too difficult or time-consuming. Practicing them will save you time, money, and heartbreaks.

Chapter 7

A Few True Heroes and Heroines – Amateur Collectors Who Created Our Cultural, Artistic and Historic Institutions

---

"The hobby of an amateur became the world's best endowed museum."
– William Wilson, author, referring to J. Paul Getty

"I have been an amateur connoisseur of art."
– Paul Mellon

"The collecting of books in the United States is virtually exclusively in the hands of leaders of business and industry. Not a single great library in the world has been formed by a great scholar."
– A.S.W. Rosenbach, rare book dealer

THIS MAY BE the most encouraging chapter.

Virtually all great American collectors have been amateurs. Their expertise and experience was in other fields, and the money they used to assemble their collections was earned working on matters far removed from the objects they were collecting. When each began, he or she knew little about the fields they had chosen to pursue. They learned on the way. And then they gave their wondrous collections to the people. In this process they created the largest and finest museum system the world has ever known. It is difficult to over-praise their accomplishments and generosity.

The root of the word "amateur" is the Latin word for "love." These amateurs spent their time, energy and money, often over several decades, to assemble the greatest treasures the world had to offer. Never in the history of humankind has there been such a determined, concentrated and generous offering. We are all the beneficiaries of their philanthropy.

American museums owe their very existence to amateurs. Docents by the thousands volunteer their time. Trustees spend time, money and energy without compensation. Ninety percent of all objects in museums came as contributions from collectors.

Here are a few words about some of the thousands of collectors who gave their collections to the people and forged the greatest museum system in the world. As you read their names it would not be inappropriate to say "thank you."

In 1638 a small college was founded on a single acre of land near Boston. At the same time a young clergyman, dying of consumption, willed his library collection of four hundred volumes to the college. It was the first library in British North America. The Massachusetts Bay Colony was so moved by this benefaction, books being rare and treasured at that time, that they named the college for him. His name was John Harvard.

Thanks to the acquisitive nature of John Trumbull, who assembled an outstanding series of paintings on the Revolutionary War in the early nineteenth century, Yale took the lead by establishing the first university art museum in 1832. Yale named it the Trumbull Gallery in honor of the paintings acquired from Trumbull. This started a trend that continues to this day, as hundreds of colleges and universities have determined the value of having a museum on campus as part of the educational process.

Ann Pamela Cunningham, distressed by the frightful condition of Mount Vernon, George Washington's home, and aware that developers were about to acquire and level it, formed the Mount Vernon Ladies Association. She roused the populace and raised the funds necessary to acquire the plantation and restore and maintain it. The association still operates Mount Vernon 137 years later and educates a million visitors a year. This was our first National Historic Preservation Society. We now have two thousand. Historic preservation societies not only save structures but scour the land for original objects to fill the homes. They are true, passionate and indispensable collectors.

James Jackson Jarves, a wealthy American who made the Grand Tour of Europe in the nineteenth century and returned with 119 quality Italian paintings, was one of our first collectors. He eventually came upon hard times and had to sell his collection. Yale University, capitalizing on its initial move with John Trumbull and convinced of the importance and value of fine art collections, bought it for $20,000. Jarves deserved recognition not for bequeathing his collection to Yale but for assembling it so early and with such a fine eye. Today it remains one of Yale's most valuable and distinguished properties and worth many times the amount paid.

The largest gift ever to the public was made by J. Paul Getty. He left almost his entire fortune, now estimated to be $5 billion, to the Getty Museum in 1976. Under the inspired leadership of Harold Williams for the past decade, the Getty Musuem has undergone the most dramatic physical development in the history of art. The new complex in Los Angeles known as Getty Center, is the costliest private project in California's experience and among the most expensive anywhere in the world to date. Sitting atop a 110-acre hill overlooking our largest city, it contains six elegant buildings housing the Getty Center for the History of Art and the Humanities, a research and study center, a center for education in the arts on all school levels, an art history information center that finds ways to use technology for the arts, a museum management training institute, a library for which 750,000 books and 60,000 photographs were acquired and the art museum itself. The cost will approximate $1 billion. Even after this huge expenditure, the trust is still valued at over $4 billion.

The Getty collection, which grows in stature every year, includes works by Titian, Rubens, Rembrandt, Renoir, Monet, Gainsborough, Raphael, Romney, Degas, Gauguin. The Getty spends more than the combined art budgets of all fifty American state governments. Its annual acquisition budget alone is five times larger than that of the National Gallery or the Metropolitan Museum.

Thomas Gilcrease was part Cree Indian, one of fourteen children. He struck oil on the 160 acres that had been assigned to him in Oklahoma, then Indian Territory, as part of a government grant program. At that time there were no museums or libraries in Oklahoma and virtually nothing was being done to preserve the records or relics of the native American culture. With his new wealth, Gilcrease set out to correct this; he acquired a remarkable collection of Indian and American art, statuary, relics, and an enormous library which he housed in the Gilcrease Institute of American History and Art in Tulsa. He wanted to preserve this story for future generations. His collection includes works by Charles Russell, Frederick Remington, Albert Jacob Miller, Albert Bierstadt, Thomas Moran and George Catlin. Without his dedication and the expenditure of practically his entire fortune, our country would not have as complete a record of these early days.

Liberty E. Holden, a schoolteacher who invested in real estate in the Great Lakes area that turned out to contain large quantities of iron ore, acquired two art collections, built his own gallery and then turned everything over to the Cleveland Museum of Art. His gifts remain among the outstanding works of art in this elegant museum. Leonard Hanna, manufacturer, supported and encouraged the Cleveland Museum of Art for decades by providing them with funds for outstanding acquisitions, his own private collection of forty nineteenth-century French pictures and his considerable estate.

Lillie P. Bliss, a founding member along with Mrs. Cornelius J. Sullivan and Mrs. John D. Rockefeller, Jr., of the Museum of Modern Art in New York, supported the effort by giving her entire unique collection of modern art. This became the nucleus for the new museum.

Mr. and Mrs. Robert Woods Bliss gave their mansion, Dumbarton Oaks in Washington, D.C., to Harvard University along with a marvelous library, extensive gardens and their collection of Byzantine and pre-Columbian art. Dumbarton Oaks has since become famous as the meeting place for the founders of the United Nations.

An oilman from Fort Worth, Texas, Amon Carter loved western art and assembled a large collection including Remingtons and Russells. He then employed Philip Johnson, the internationally known architect, to design a pristine building to house the collection. Carter's daughter Ruth Carter Johnson assumed control and enlarged the Amon Carter Museum of Western Art's interests to include a wider range of Americana.

Anne and Amy Putnam acquired one of the finest collection of Old Masters in the western United States. They were determined to keep the paintings in San Diego, their home, and appealed to Henry Timken, a friend and a member of the Timken roller-bearing family. He, too, considered San Diego home. Henry agreed and built the Timken Art Gallery in 1965 to house the Putnams' collection. It has been called "a jewel box for the arts"; this is as it should be, for the works rank with the world's finest.

One of the earliest research libraries in America was established by Walter Loomis Newberry, a Chicago real estate operator in the late nineteenth century. It has such a diverse collection that its motto is "an uncommon collection of uncommon collections." Today, after a century of service, its collection is still expanding and its usage by scholars increases every year.

A Few True Heroes and Heroines

John Carter Brown of Providence, Rhode Island, assembled the premier collection of books on the discovery, exploration and settlement of the New World, then built a library to house the collection and endowed the library. The Brown Library continues to draw scholars from around the world and the collection is added to continuously.

Henry Ford built his museum in Dearborn, Michigan to exhibit a wide range of Americana including vintage automobiles, Edison's laboratory and a one-room schoolhouse. Generations of children have visited and learned. Now a new charter school for 100 Detroit students has been built.

James Lenox, a bachelor and contemporary competitor for rare books with John Carter Brown, dedicated his life to his library. His collection became the core for the New York Public Library. It was of Lenox, among others, that Bernard McTigue, keeper of rare books at the library said, "Institutional libraries would not exist as we know them if it were not for private collectors. They have always been the people who put the pieces together. It is their passion that builds these collections."

The Crear Library was founded by John Crear as a scientific library for research in the late 1890s. It has served such an important role to business and industry as well as educators that it is now a part of the University of Chicago library system.

David Adler, a renowned architect, left his drawings and plans to the Art Institute of Chicago and thus encouraged many other area architects to do the same. Today the museum has an architectural department that preserves the plans for many of Chicago's historic buildings and makes them available for remodeling and restoration projects.

Charles Frye moved from Iowa to Seattle, started a successful meat-packing business and began collecting paintings by German artists. Upon his death, as directed by his will, his collection became the basis of a museum that was to be always free to the public. Frye and his wife, Emma, provided the funds, the endowment and the art. Over the years the collection has been added to. In 1996 the trustees completed a renovation and expansion of the building to hold the growing collection. While small and specialized, the Charles and Emma Frye Museum has fulfilled every requirement of the founder—and the public loves it.

Another meat packer, Frederick Layton, assembled Milwaukee's first art collection and then built its first museum. Merging later with the Milwaukee Art Institute, which was founded after Layton's museum, the two are now housed in a dramatic lakefront building designed by Eero Saarinen. It all started with the amateur Layton.

Elise S. Haas, heiress to the Levi Strauss clothing fortune, was the principal benefactor of San Francisco's Museum of Modern Art, now in a dramatic new building to house its collection, much of which came from Mrs. Haas. Because of her devotion and ability, Haas served as the first woman president of the museum. In addition to her gifts of art she endowed the museum and established the conservation laboratory, which ranks among the leading centers for the preservation and treatment of modern art.

Henry E. Huntington, of the famous Southern Pacific railroad dynasty, did more for preserving priceless treasures than any other member of his family. He built the Huntington Library in San Marino, California, to hold 5,300 volumes of books and manuscripts from the fifteenth century, known as incunabula. He was so determined to create the very best in its field that he acquired entire collections so that he could reach his goal more quickly. The Huntington Library is the equal of any institution in America on the subject British literature. Adjoining it are a small, intimate art museum and elegant gardens that are open to the public. Huntington made this extraordinary contribution to education without ever having attended college.

Paul and Alisa Mellon, children of Andrew Mellon, not only carried on the family's tradition of support for the arts but broke new ground as well. Paul gave Yale University the Yale Center for British Art to house his extraordinary collection, which ranks among the top three of British art in the world with 1,600 oils and over 5,000 watercolors and drawings. Paul also has given generously to the Virginia Museum of Art. But perhaps the most significant contributions Paul and Alisa have made to the American public was their continuing support of the National Gallery. As collectors increasingly sent their treasures to the gallery, it became obvious that it must be expanded. Andrew Mellon's children stepped forward and donated $100 million to build the new wing. They have also continued to give works from their collections.

Among the most generous patrons of the arts has been the Rockefeller family, who have shared their oil fortune with Americans. In all, the Rockefellers have given away more than $2 billion in support of the arts, education, research and historic sites. The greatest family contributor was John D. Rockefeller, Jr. On land he owned in New York City he constructed the Cloisters to house a museum of medieval art, which opened in 1938. Rockefeller supplied everything, including tapestries and historic windows, doors and rooms for authenticity, and endowed it with $10 million. To protect its Hudson River view, he acquired land on the New Jersey side of river and gave it to the Palisades Interstate Park Commission. In addition to the Cloisters, Rockefeller paid for restoring Versailles, Fontainebleau and the Cathedral of Rheims. He also founded the Williamsburg restoration and spent over $60 million on it alone.

Nelson, the Rockefeller family's leading politician, was perhaps the most prolific collector amongst John D. Rockefeller, Jr.'s children. He was fond of sculpture, pre-Columbian and Peruvian art and modern and contemporary art. Nelson Rockefeller established in New York the Museum of Primitive Art, now combined with the Metropolitan Museum of Art. He served as president, a trustee and a major contributor to the Museum of Modern Art in New York City, of which his mother, Mrs. John D. Rockefeller, Jr., was one of the founding members. His sister-in-law, Mrs. John D. Rockefeller) III, served two terms as president. Other members of the family and in-laws also were and are supporters of the arts and education.

Another family affair was the creation of the H.O. Havemeyer Collection, which includes several Rembrandts, El Greco, Goya, Manet, Degas, Courbet, Cézanne and Poussin pictures. Henry and Louisine Havemeyer and their son, Horace, left nearly 4,500 works of art to the Metropolitan Museum of Art. Henry made his fortune as head of the American Sugar Trust; Louisine interested him in collecting art rather late in his life. Their daughter, Electra Havemeyer Webb, founded the Shelburne Museum in Vermont to house her Americana collection of some 125,000 objects and an outstanding collection of North American big game—she was a hunter as well as a collector and philanthropist.

In addition to being the largest private supporter of education in America, Walter Annenberg, the fabulous California and Philadelphia publisher and art collector, has bequeathed his $1 billion art collection to the Metropolitan Museum of Art. It includes works by Cézanne, Van Gogh, Gauguin, Braque, Picasso, Vuillard. Other museums, including the Philadelphia Museum of Art, also received gifts of art from Annenberg. His sister Janet Annenberg Hooker gave the Smithsonian a rare jewel collection which is exhibited in a gallery named for her. She also supported renovations made in the White House.

Philip and Muriel Berman gave their outstanding collection of old masters and contemporary art along with funds to acquire art to the Philadelphia Museum of Art. He served as president of the museum for many years.

Kate, Clarence and Lucy Buckingham donated to the Art Institute of Chicago 9,500 pieces, including Asian art, Gothic items, Japanese prints and drawings. They also gave the city of Chicago the majestic Buckingham fountain, the centerpiece of the fabulous lakefront park that is Chicago's front door.

Claribel and Etta Cone, sisters from Baltimore, spent years living in France, where they became intimate friends with Matisse and other artists. During this period and for all of their adult lives they collected paintings—more than fifty from Matisse alone, enough to form one of the world's great collections of the work of this artist. Upon their deaths, the collection was given to the Baltimore Museum of Art, which built a new wing to house it. It is the jewel of the museum.

Henry Clay Frick's New York City mansion became the Frick Collection to house his 2,300 works of art. His collection included Rembrandt's *Polish Rider*, Chardin's *Still Life with Plums* and three Vermeers. Frick, a close friend of Andrew Mellon's (both grew up in Pittsburgh), made his fortune as a partner of Andrew Carnegie in the steel industry.

Isabella Stewart Gardner built her own museum in Boston in the style of an Italianate palazzo as a memorial to herself and to exhibit her collection. She had over a half-dozen portraits of herself painted by Sargent, Whistler and others. Gardner depended on Bernard Berenson to guide her acquisitions. Her will stipulated that no changes could be made in her museum.

The newspaper and magazine publisher William Randolph Hearst perhaps bought more objects than anyone else. At one time he is reputed to have been responsible for 25 percent of all art purchases in the world. Hearst's mother, Phoebe, actually started him on his colossal collecting splurges. Lord Duveen called Hearst a "gatherer" rather than a collector, and hard financial times forced him to sell much of what he had bought; nevertheless, he was a benefactor to many museums and other institutions. The Los Angeles County Museum of Art was one his chief beneficiaries; his gifts helped the museum develop a more independent status rather than continuing only as an adjunct of the Museum of History and Science. His fabulous castle in California, which his family gave to the state, has more visitors and income than any other state park.

Marjorie Merriweather Post, heiress of the Post Cereal fortune, left the nation her home, "Hillwood," in Washington, D.C., together with a collection of Imperial Russian paintings, decorative arts, French furniture and porcelain and a six-thousand-volume library. One of her husbands had been ambassador to Russia, which allowed them to acquire Russian art during the 1930s.

Jo Ann and Julian Ganz, Los Angeles, have what many consider the finest collection of nineteenth-century American paintings in private hands. It includes works by Homer, Bellows, Sargent, Church and many others. Part of their collection has been promised to the National Gallery, and the Los Angeles County Museum of Art hopes to be a beneficiary as well.

Edgar and Bernice Chrysler Garbisch assembled a collection of hundreds of American folk paintings and primitive art from the eighteenth and nineteenth centuries. He was an Army officer. They started collecting when they purchased a few American Folk pictures to brighten their home in Maryland. Then they were off, leading to a collection of 2,500 objects. They distributed portions of their large collection to many museums including the National Gallery, the Metropolitan Museum, the Philadelphia Museum and many smaller museums.

Several members of the famous and wealthy Guggenheim mining family were outstanding collectors. In the early part of this century, Solomon Guggenheim assembled the greatest collection of nonobjective art then in existence, which included works by Kandinsky, Bauer and Moholy-Nagy. As his collection grew, he determined to build his own museum, which he did in New York, employing Frank Lloyd Wright to design the world-famous Solomon R. Guggenheim Museum. It has been a great success and recently completed a major expansion.

His niece Peggy Guggenheim, an expatriate born in New York, became interested in art at early age and collected the newest and most contemporary examples. Finally settled in her Palazzo Venier dei Leoni on the Grand Canal in Venice, Italy, which became an important port of call for collectors, she had many lovers, some of whom were artists. Her collection includes works by Dali, Ernst, Tanguy, Duchamp, Pollock, Picasso, Rothko, Diego Rivera, Brancusi, Calder and Giacometti as well as a selection of pre-Columbian and primitive art. She opened her palazzo to the public and toward the end of her life she left the collection and the palazzo to her uncle's museum in New York City.

Mrs. Potter Palmer, Chicago's society leader and the wife of one of the leaders of nineteenth-century Chicago (the builder of the famous Palmer House Hotel), became interested in art collecting through her friendship with Mary Cassatt, who advised her. Mrs. Palmer was among the earliest acquirers of French Impressionist artists and gave much of her collection, including works by Renoir, Monet and Pissarro, to the Art Institute of Chicago. Her son, Potter Palmer, Jr., and her granddaughter's husband were both presidents of the museum.

One of Paul Sachs's Harvard disciples, Henry P. McIlhenny came from a family of collectors and supporters of the Philadelphia Museum of Art. His father and sister served as president and Henry himself was curator of decorative arts for thirty years. He left his collection of works by Renoir, Degas, Matisse, Delacroix and others to the Philadelphia museum.

Dr. Alfred C. Barnes developed Argyrol antiseptic and thus made a fortune. He became an avid collector, early on acquiring works by Cézanne, Renoir, Degas, Matisse, Picasso, Van Gogh, Modigliani, Soutine, Seurat, Monet, Manet, Courbet, Klee, Utrillo and Braque, among others. He called them "The Old Masters of the future." He was probably right. Dr. Barnes also collected sculpture. Using the dealer Paul Guillaume extensively, he made many of his acquisitions at the depth of the Great Depression of the 1930s, when masterpieces were available at very low prices. Dr. Barnes built and endowed his own gallery in the Philadelphia suburb of Merion to house his collection. After his death in an automobile accident a few miles from his home, his entire collection went to the Barnes Foundation. His will was very restrictive as to the dispensation of his works and regarding when and how visitors were welcome in the gallery. At times it appeared that Dr. Barnes did not like anyone.

Charles L. Blockson was such an outstanding athlete at Pennsylvania State Univerity that the New York Giants football team offered him a contract. But Blockson had other plans—namely, to be a "black bibliophile" and to work at bringing together the greatest collection on black history in America. Starting his own business in Philadelphia and then entering education, Blockson collected over twenty thousand books, manuscripts, pamphlets and writings, which later became part of the library of Temple University in Philadelphia. Blockson went with the collection as curator and continued to build the library until it now exceeds eighty thousand items. It is probably the largest and most extensive collection on black history in America. Without his determination and dedication, much of this material would be far gone by now.

Phillip and Robert Lehman's enormous art collection was given to Metropolitan Museum of Art which built a 25,000-square-foot pavilion to permanently exhibit it. The pavilion is a reconstruction of the rooms that housed the collection in the Lehman residence. The collection, which included paintings by Rembrandt and El Greco, had been started by the father, Philip, who had founded the investment banking company Lehman Brothers. At the time of his death in 1969, Robert, the son, had what many considered the greatest collection still in private hands. He left to the museum three thousand works of art valued then at $100,000,000—but in actuality priceless.

Andrew Carnegie, the steel tycoon who was at the time the richest man in the world, built hundreds of free public libraries to stimulate reading and education, particularly in our crowded urban cities. No such attempt had ever been made before. He also founded the first art museum in Pittsburgh.

Duncan Phillips, yet another steel baron from Pittsburgh, was encouraged by his wife, Marjorie, an artist, to collect art. Together they built a collection consisting of works by Daumier, El Greco, Braque, Bonnard, Hartley, Eakins, Renoir. Their collection is now an independent museum in Washington, D.C., known as the Phillips Collection.

Casino magnate William Harrah collected classic automobiles. He built the National Automobile Museum in Reno, Nevada, which exhibits more than two hundred antique automobiles.

In order to capture the essence of early America, Henry Ford acquired eighty historic sites, including one of Thomas Edison's laboratories, and moved them to Dearborn, Michigan, where he created the Henry Ford Museum and Greenfield Village. In addition to the buildings themselves, the museum and village contain a million historical artifacts.

Benjamin Altman, the department store magnate, collected Chinese porcelains and Old Masters. A reclusive bachelor who lived quite frugally, Altman dedicated his wealth to his collection. He owned more Rembrandts than any other American collector. Altman left his entire collection to the Metropolitan Museum of Art. Known as the Altman Collection, it had nearly one thousand top-quality objects valued at $15 million in 1913. At the time, it was the largest gift ever given to the museum.

Avery Brundage, an engineer who served as president of the International Olympic Committee for twenty years, collected)cisco.

John C. Dorrance, of the family that founded the Campbell Soup Company, collected soup tureens and created the Campbell Soup Museum to house and exhibit them. Later the family gave the collection of 250 objects to the Winterthur Museum.

Mr. and Mrs. Kay Kimbell, he an oil and commodities broker, left an art collection and $100 million for construction of a museum in Fort Worth, Texas, to house it. The result is one of the most beautiful of modern structures, and the enlarged collection today is recognized worldwide.

A nineteenth-century collector who assembled the largest collection of books and manuscripts ever, known as Bibliotheca Phillippica, Sir Thomas Phillips was driven to own one copy of every book ever published. After his death it took Sotheby's nearly a century and sixty separate sales to auction off his complete library. American book collectors were among the largest purchasers at the auctions.

Henry F. du Pont created Winterthur Museum in his former home, which had been the family residence for generations, having been built in 1839. It has had to be expanded three times to accommodate the volume of books and American decorative objects and the installation of more than 125 period rooms. The collections contain American furniture, paintings, textiles and sculpture and a 150,000-volume library of books, manuscripts and photographs. It is the most magnificent collection of Americana in existence and it is open to the public year round.

Sterling and Francine Clark, heirs to the Singer Sewing Machine Company, assembled a collection of Renoir paintings and created the Sterling and Francine Clark Art Institute in Williamstown, Massachusetts, to house them. The founders themselves, who bought most of their art from dealers M. Knoedler and Durand-Ruel, are also housed in the museum; their bodies are buried in an area near the front entrance.

John and Mable Ringling, the circus impresarios, built a large Italian Renaissance museum in Sarasota, Florida, next to the mansion in which they lived. It contains what is probably America's finest collection of Baroque and Rococo art, including several Rubens paintings, plus the Ringling Circus Museum. They bequeathed the entire compound to the state of Florida for the enjoyment of the people. No other museum can quite compare to the Ringling.

Henry N. Flynt saved Historic Deerfield, Massachusetts, by acquiring thirteen eighteenth- and nineteenth-century residential structures, including their contents, and restoring them to their original condition. This unusual collection encompasses paintings, furniture, ceramics, costumes, and other decorative arts, all of which are from the frontier period.

A Detroit manufacturer of railroad cars, Charles Lang Freer collected Oriental art and works by James McNeill Whistler, including his remarkable "Peacock Room." Freer gave his collection of 4,811 objects to the Smithsonian Institution and funded a building now named the Freer Gallery. At the time, his collection was estimated to be worth $7 million and the building $1 million. Today's values would be many times these figures. The museum opened in 1923 in Washington, D.C. Unfortunately, Freer had died in 1919, so he never saw his collection installed in its own gallery.

Arthur Alfonso Schomburg, born in Puerto Rico, set out to document the history of the black race. Although he spent most of his career in banking with a modest income, collecting was his passion and first priority. Over the years he assembled an outstanding collection, which he sold to the New York Public Library and then eventually became its curator. He continued to build the record. The Schomburg Collection has become a primary source of information on the history of the black experience in America.

Wilhelmina Cole Holladay was so determined that women artists should be recognized that she raised $15 million, bought a building and gave her own collection to the cause. It is because of her generosity that the National Museum of Women in the Arts now stands in Washington, D.C.

Gertrude Vanderbilt Whitney, heiress and sculptor, founded the Whitney Museum of American Art in 1930 in New York City. Earlier she had offered her collection plus an endowment and money to build a wing to the Metropolitan but was turned down, as there was not much appreciation for modern art among the trustees at the moment. At the same time, other New Yorkers were forming the Museum of Modern Art. Modern and contemporary art was about to move into the American art scene in a big way. But Whitney did not limit her interests to modern art. The Buffalo Bill Historical Center in Cody, Wyoming, is there because of her. Whitney acquired the large piece of land on which the center sits, sculpted the heroic-sized statue of Buffalo Bill that greets one at the entrance and gave funds for construction.

Unbeknown to most people, Buffalo Bill had a substantial collection of western art. When he fell upon bad times late in his life, he was forced to sell his collection. Mr. and Mrs. Paul C. Newell acquired it and gave it to the museum—another thoughtful act of private philanthropy that helped preserve for all of us a significant piece of our history and culture.

James E. Scripps, of the newspaper family, gave the Detroit Institute of Arts seventy Old Master paintings in 1889. At that time, this raised the institute to the forefront with other major museums and became the linchpin for the successful growth in size and quality that has followed.

Members of another newspaper family, Mr. and Mrs. Joseph Pulitzer, Jr., gave to the St. Louis Art Museum some of the most valuable and widely recognized works of art in its possession.

In 1900 John J. Albright financed the entire cost of a new building for an art gallery in Buffalo, New York. His initial generosity stimulated a flow of art and money to the new museum from many others in the community, most notably Seymour H. Knox, who gave hundreds of works of art. The museum, world-renowned for its collection of modern and contemporary art, is now known as the Albright-Knox Art Gallery.

The city of Chicago has benefited enormously over the years from the generosity of the Field family. Marshall Field, the premier retailer at the turn of the century, built and endowed the city's world-famous Field Museum of Natural History. It would be impossible to duplicate the extraordinary collections today. His nephew Stanley ran the museum for three decades with distinction. His great-great-grandson, Marshall Field V, has enlarged the Field traditon of public service by serving as chairman of the Art Institute of Chicago for two terms, giving paintings from his fine art collection and funds to build a new wing for American art. Chicago would not be the cultural center that it is today without them.

Henry Clay Folger and Emily Jordan Folger assembled a masterful collection of Shakespeare's works and gave them to the people along with the Folger Shakespeare Library in Washington, D.C. Their ashes are kept near the reading room.

August Heckscher, a German immigrant who earned his fortune in America, gave the city of Huntington, New York, a five-winged marble museum building and a park to go with it in appreciation of all that America had given him.

A Philadelphia lawyer who served J. P. Morgan and other corporate and financial leaders at the turn of the century, John G. Johnson collected French, Spanish, Flemish and American works of art in his spare time. He left 1,200 objects to the Philadelphia Museum of Art.

Leigh and Mary Block, he a member of the Inland Steel Company family, started collecting in 1942 and assembled works from Van Gogh, Cézanne, Degas, Braque, Fragonard, Picasso and others. They left the bulk of their collection to the Art Institute of Chicago, where Leigh had been president. Gifts were also made to the Santa Barbara Museum of Art and Northwestern University.

Wright S. Ludington spent his lifetime as a collector of wide-ranging objects from antiquity to contemporary paintings and sculpture. A founder of the Santa Barbara Museum of Art in 1941, he was the largest and most generous donor to the museum. His collection included works by Rodin, Derain, Modigliani and Rousseau and Greek and Roman sculpture and relics.

The generosity of Edward Drummond Libbey, glass manufacturer, made the Toledo Museum of Art one of the finest in the country. Among his gifts was a collection of five thousand pieces of ancient glass. He and his wife left their entire fortunes to the Ohio museum with the stipulation that 50 percent be used for operations and 50 percent for acquisitions.

Katherine Sophie Drier became a fearless and outspoken advocate of modern art at the turn of the century when there were few followers. She did everything possible to promote the new art, including speaking, writing articles, forming committees, finding and supporting new artists and arguing with anyone who disagreed with her. Drier culminated her long struggle by awarding her collection of modern art to Yale University, believing that they were in a position to advance the cause.

Mrs. Eugene Fuller and her son Richard built and gave to the city of Seattle a marvelous museum and their outstanding Oriental art collection. Richard served as both president and director for many years. The Seattle Art Museum has flourished ever since.

Joseph R. Hirshhorn, born in Latvia to a poor family, once stated, "I've known starvation, what it is to survive on garbage." He became a mining tycoon and assembled a vast collection consisting of thousands of contemporary paintings and sculpture. He gave most of his collection to the Smithsonian Institution, which built the Hirshhorn Museum and Sculpture Garden.

Generations of families have enjoyed the generosity of the Preston Morton family of Morton Salt fame. The Mortons left magnificent collections to the Art Institute of Chicago and the Santa Barbara Museum of Art and created and gave to the people the Morton Arboretum on thousands of acres just west of Chicago.

George Gustav Heye, an engineer operating in the western United States, amassed 4,500,000 Native American relics and founded the Museum of the American Indian in New York City, now part of the Smithsonian Institution.

Chauncey and Brooks McCormick, father and son farm equipment and truck manufacturers, left many works to museums and served for decades on the board of the Art Insitute of Chicago. Brooks, along with Marshall Field, funded the museum's new American art gallery.

William Rockhill Nelson, owner and publisher of the Kansas City *Star*, left his substantial wealth to his wife and daughter with the stipulation that upon their deaths the fortune in its entirety would be given to an art foundation to create and endow a museum for Kansas City. Mary M. Atkins also left a fortune for the use of a museum. Between the two of them, Kansas City constructed the Nelson-Atkins Museum, a wonderful structure with a marvelous collection.

Charles Wrightsman, an oil millionaire, and his wife, Jayne, became avid collectors. They acquired Old Masters, porcelains, furniture and Impressionist paintings and gave the bulk of their collection to the Metropolitan Museum of Art.

Klaus G. and Amelia Perls gave their outstanding collection of twentieth-century art, valued at $60 million, to the Metropolitan Museum in 1996. The Perlses are Manhattan dealers and collectors.

Dominique de Menil of Houston founded the Menil Collection, consisting of ten thousand works of Cubists, Surrealists, and contemporary art as well as African sculpture and Mediterranean antiquities. It also contains a library of some twenty thousand volumes. Born in France, she became a U.S. citizen.

William H. Scheide, who is said to have the finest privately owned rare book collection in North America, represents the third generation to develop and care for this monumental collection. His grandfather, in business with John D. Rockefeller, retired at an early age in western Pennsylvania and started collecting books that contained important information. His son, in turn, added to the collection, bringing many rare volumes and manuscripts from Europe. William Scheide has continued the family tradition by caring for the library he inherited and adding another third to it. It now stands at about five thousand items representing 130 years of collecting by the same family. By special arrangement with Princeton University, where William and his father matriculated, he constructed at his expense a private room atop the Firestone Library to house the collection and to serve as his office. He employs a librarian, also at his expense. In his eighties, he is still a dedicated collector. While the collection remains privately owned, scholars are permitted to use it. There is as yet no understanding between Scheide and Princeton as to the final disposition of his library. Time alone will tell. Regardless of his final decision, the family has been responsible for bringing to America hundreds of rare books and manuscripts that would not be here except for them.

Mrs. James Ward Thorne, a homemaker with no training in interior design, architecture or the arts, created her world-famous miniature Thorne rooms which are now permanently exhibited at the Art Institute of Chicago and have been one of the most popular attractions for generations. There is nothing else quite like them.

Two railroaders, William Walters and his son Henry, gathered a prodigious collection of Old Masters, Roman antiquities, sculpture, manuscripts, Chinese porcelains—in all more than four thousand works. They were among the first American collectors of Oriental objects. The entire collection was given to the city of Baltimore, which built an appropriate museum building for the Walters Art Gallery.

Thomas B. Walker, a lumberman with a fiercely independent nature, turned his home into Minneapolis's first art gallery as his collection grew. This stimulated others to launch a second art center and Clinton Morrison gave the land to form the Minneapolis Institute of Art. Eventually, his family gave a fine collection and large amounts of money to the institute. William H. Dinwoody and family also left a fortune for the acquisition of art. The Walker Art Center, under the direction of Thomas's granddaughter, greatly expanded its area of interest and is now considered Minneapolis's equivalent of New York's Museum of Modern Art. Minneapolis has been richly endowed and well served by its private collectors.

The story of the Widener family is one of dedication, passion, tragedy and final fulfillment. Young Harry Elkins Widener, son of a wealthy Philadelphia family, collected rare books, his ambition being "to be remembered in connection with a great library." He and his parents traveled to England on a book-buying expedition and returned on the *Titanic*. The young man and his father were lost at sea. His mother, Mrs. George Widener, determined to carry out his dream, built the Harry Elkins Widener Memorial Library at Harvard University, her son's alma mater, to house his collection. It became Harvard's core library.

The Harvard libraries, totally supported by private philanthropy, contain 13 million volumes, the most in the nation.

Charles Wright, a physician, founded the original Museum of African American history in Detroit in 1965. The museum has since moved to a new and much expanded facility. Although he is no longer connected with it, without Dr. Wright's initial efforts it is questionable that the new museum would have been possible.

Where would we be without the vision and generosity of these individuals?

Chapter 8

Collecting for History – How Our Most Important Presidential Sites Were Saved

---

"Here, it's always been possible for the most ordinary person to become the most powerful one in the world. The epic distance between the White House and the birthplace is something uniquely American."

– Edmund Morris, author and historian

"The papers of the Presidents are among the most valuable sources of material for history. They ought to be preserved, and ought to be used."

– Harry S. Truman, 33rd President of the United States

BEFORE PRESIDENTIAL LIBRARIES came into being, their papers and mementos were dispersed and often lost or destroyed. It was not until Franklin D. Roosevelt donated his personal and presidential papers to the people through the federal government that the presidential library system was established.

Perhaps it was Roosevelt's knowledge and sense of history that led him to become the first president to do so. He knew the tremendous interest we Americans have in the history of our country and the pride we take in our finest achievements. The examples set by Mount Vernon and Monticello were enough to prove that a more deliberate and sure way of saving our presidential sites and records had to be created. At the same time Roosevelt gave land on his Hyde Park, New York, estate for the building of an appropriate library and museum. Admirers formed a non-profit organization to raise the necessary funds.

Completed in 1946, the library and museum were so popular that a few years later Congress passed the Presidential Libraries Act by which all future presidents would be able to donate their personal and presidential papers and mementos, thus ensuring that they would be preserved for all time and be made available to the people. The act stipulated that the libraries were to be constructed with private funds, after which the National Archives would operate and maintain them.

Since then nine additional presidential libraries have been contructed. The George Bush Presidential Library and Museum is the latest to be completed. The seventy-thousand-square-foot building opened in 1997 on a ninety-acre site on the campus of Texas A & M University in College Station, Texas. It houses forty million documents and memorabilia. The total cost was $83 million, all raised from private donors.

Richard Nixon's records are under hold because of the Watergate controversy, although a Library has been opened along with his birthplace in Yorba Linda, California. A fund-raising campaign for the construction of Bill Clinton's library and museum started during his second term. The ten existing presidential libraries and the two projects still to be completed hold 250 million pages of records, correspondence and textual materials, 5 million photographs, 13 million feet of motion picture film, 70 hours of recordings and nearly 300,000 museum objects.

It may seem surprising that it took Congress so long to establish the Presidential Libraries Act, but then the federal government has never been zealous about matters such as this. It has always rested on the private citizen and collectors to save our most precious historical objects and sites.

81

In Praise of America's Collectors

The tale of George Washington's Mount Vernon illustrates this rather dramatically. Washington's home had been in his family since 1674, when George's great-grandfather John Washington gained title to the Mount Vernon site. George's father, Augustine, then occupied it. In 1754 George took title to it. He left Mount Vernon initially to lead our nation's struggle for independence in the Revolutionary War and for the second time when he was elected our first president. Following his presidency, Washington had only two and a half years to enjoy Mount Vernon before his death in 1799. Some time later descendents offered the mansion and land to the federal government, which refused it. Then, just as developers were to acquire the site, private citizens stepped forward. In 1858 the Mount Vernon Ladies Association of the Union, led by Ann Pamela Cunningham, raised the funds to purchase the mansion and several outbuildings on five hundred acres and to restore the buildings and grounds. Thanks to devoted collectors, the mansion contains much of the furniture, paintings and other works of art that were originally in place, as well as the desk and chair that Washington used in his president's office. His library contained 884 volumes, of which 75 originals remain, having been returned to the mansion over the years by individuals. The President and Mrs. Washington's bedchamber, still containing the bed in which he died, is on the second floor. His and Mrs. Washington's tomb is on the estate. Mount Vernon is now designated a National Historic Landmark and receives a million visitors a year. The Mount Vernon Ladies Association still manages and maintains the property.

Later, in 1923, Washington's birthplace, which is in the same general area, was recovered by the Wakefield National Memorial Association. Although all the buildings had been destroyed by fire and time, the association determined to resurrect the site and funded the purchase of 394 acres surrounding the site of Washington's birth. A memorial house and colonial garden have been built, and in 1932, the 200th anniversary of George Washington's birth, the park was opened to the public and its title transferred to the federal government.

Mount Vernon and Washington's birthplace have been preserved due to the diligence and generosity of thousands of individuals who gave of their time, money and skills to save for all Americans the birth site and residence of the founder of our country and our first president. It could happen only in America.

Thomas Jefferson's Monticello is another case. Jefferson designed, built and lived in this home all his adult life until his death at age eighty-three in 1826. He planned every building and the gardens as well. Many of his possessions, including a portion of his library, are still intact and in his home. Following his death, members of his family struggled to maintain the large home and estate but were unsuccessful, in part because Jefferson had died nearly penniless and owing large sums. With time, the magnificent house and grounds fell into disrepair. In 1923, private citizens organized the Thomas Jefferson Memorial Foundation, a non-profit organization, which now owns the house, gardens and some two thousand acres on Jefferson's mountaintop. The gardens have been completely restored in accordance with Jefferson's original plans.

Abraham Lincoln, acclaimed by many historians to be our greatest president, lived a life well known to all Americans. His birthplace in Hodgenville, Kentucky, has been preserved and honored by a handsome memorial building built on the site of the Lincoln family's farm and cabin. The cabin itself has been moved and erected within the building. The memorial was built with funds raised by popular subscription, mostly by school children. Some three hundred thousand people visit the cabin each year.

Lincoln's home in Springfield, Illinois, where he lived when elected president, was acquired and restored by the Abraham Lincoln Association of Springfield and the National Society of the Colonial Dames in Illinois. It is now a National Historic Site. Salem Village, Illinois, where Lincoln lived for several years and clerked in the local store, was acquired and restored by William Randolph Hearst and given to the people. All the Lincoln residences were saved, restored and preserved by private efforts, and all are open to the public without charge.

The Adams National Historic Site, birthplaces of both John Adams and John Quincy Adams, our second and sixth presidents, is in Quincy, Massachusetts. The two houses are within walking distance of each other on the same street. Furnishings from their extraordinary careers, including many books from each, populate the homes. The balance of John Adams's library was given to the Boston Public Library in 1893 by the family. The Adams families continued to live in the houses long after the two presidents had died. The birthplaces were eventually acquired by the city of Quincy, which presented them to the federal government. In 1946 the Adamses presented to the government a third nearby residence that had been occupied by the family for generations. It was given with the stipulation that it was for the American people.

Andrew Jackson's home, known as the Hermitage, is located in Nashville, Tennessee, on 625 acres. He first built it in 1828 and then rebuilt a grander home when the original house burned to the ground. Jackson died at the Hermitage, and he and his wife are buried on the grounds. It was in desolate condition when the Ladies Hermitage Association saved and preserved it. The mansion is furnished with original pieces the Jacksons owned and with many items of interest from his White House days, thanks to the generosity of family members and collectors. The Hermitage, too, is open to the public.

James Madison, our fourth president, had the most unusual living experience of any of our presidents. The British burned the White House while he was president, and he and his family were forced to live elsewhere in temporary quarters. The home that is preserved is the famous Octagon, a three-story brick residence in Washington, D.C., named for its design. For years after the Madisons left, the building gradually went downhill, being used for various purposes with little care. Because of its unique design, the American Institute of Architects acquired it in 1899 as their national headquarters. Under the discerning eyes of the architects it has been restored to its former glory and is meticulously maintained, including the gardens, which have been rebuilt. It is open to the public without charge.

Upon Madison's retirement, the family acquired a home in Montpelier Station, Virginia, where they lived until their deaths. The residence changed hands several times and was then acquired by William duPont, who enlarged it and operated the grounds as a plantation. In 1984 the duPonts deeded it to the National Trust for Historic Preservation and opened it to the public.

Theodore Roosevelt's birthplace and library in New York City and Sagamore Hill, Oyster Bay, New York, which he built and where he lived his adult life and died, are both preserved and open to the public. The family and admirers of Roosevelt have contributed funds, objects and time. The properties are administered by the Theodore Roosevelt Association.

James Monroe's residence, Ash Lawn in Charlottesville, Virginia, is on a 535-acre working farm. It was acquired by Jay and Helen Johns in 1931 and later bequeathed to William and Mary College as "an historic shrine for the education of the general public."

Several other presidential birthplaces have been preserved through gifts from the family or other private funds. Herbert Hoover's family renovated the Quaker cottage in West Branch, Iowa, where he was born, and gave it to the nation. The United Auto Workers acquired Harry Truman's birthplace and gave it to the government. Dwight Eisenhower's family gave the home in which he was born to the country. John F. Kennedy's family acquired his birthplace, restored and refurnished it with original pieces and gave it to the nation. Lyndon Johnson's birthplace was also restored by his family and given to the United States.

Saving presidential sites is only part of the drive to preserve our historic past. There are two thousand active historic preservation societies, with more being formed every year. They are finders, savers, and holders of some of our most precious documents and artifacts. The private National Trust for Historic Preservation has done a herculean job of identifying and saving many buildings that have played an important role in the development and history of America. With 250,000 dues-paying members who subscribe to its regularly published magazine, the trust calls the public's attention to scores of buldings worthy of saving by publishing a list of our most endangered historic places every year. They own and operate eighteen, including three presidential sites, for the benefit of the public.

Many other presidential sites have also been preserved. These are only a few examples. Our presidential histories live on thanks to the generosity of the people.

Chapter 9

Unusual Collectors and Collections – The Passions and Acquisitions of Some Unconventional Americans

---

"It doesn't take a fortune to put together a great collection."

– Edward Akeley, collector

"Where would history and biography be unless there were collectors?"

– Carl Sandburg, Pulitzer Prize-winning biographer of Abraham Lincoln

THE COLLECTORS AND MUSEUMS in this chapter demonstrate how rewarding a collecting idea can be, even if—or perhaps especially if—it is out of the ordinary or the collector goes to extremes to feed his or her passion. The list expands continuously as new collectors discover themes of interest and value. There appears to be no limit.

Anna and Edward Akeley, of Lafayette, Indiana, collected German paintings, Japanese woodblock prints and Latin American art for decades. They lived rather frugal lives to help pay for the art they bought. After Edward died at age eighty-nine, Anna gave their collection away, in accordance with his wishes. The

University of Chicago, where he had earned his Ph.D., Purdue University, which he had attended, and the University of South Dakota, where his father had headed the engineering department, were the beneficiaries. The collection was valued at over $1 million; Anna estimated they had spent only about $30,000 in all. She summed up their experience by stating, "Edward showed it doesn't take a fortune to put together a great collection."

George Arents, Jr., collected everything possible about tobacco, the source of his income, including 125,000 cigarette cards. He gave the entire collection to the New York Public Library along with an endowment.

Ruth Baldwin, a professor with three degrees, spent a lifetime assembling a library of over 100,000 children's books, eventually giving them to the University of Florida when they agreed to her being the curator of her collection. One of her associates observed, "The hunt is everything for her. It was the excitement of finding and getting it. It was the one consuming passion in her life."

George Barris collects cars made famous by the movies, most of which he designed and created. They include the Batmobile, James Bond's BMW Z-3 from the *Golden Eye* production and the *Dukes of Hazard*'s red 1969 Dodge Charger. They are exhibited in the Star Cars Museum, Gatlinburg, Tennessee.

Helen and Robert Cargo collected three hundred Alabama-made quilts and gave them to the Birmingham Museum of Art.

Rudolph Leopold, an ophthalmologist practicing in Vienna, created the world's outstanding collection of Austrian art, starting fifty years ago. As the value of his collection grew, he borrowed from banks to buy more. By 1994, Sotheby's valued his collection at $650 million, but Leopold found himself in financial trouble due to loans from banks and overdue taxes. He worked out a deal whereby he received $75 million in cash, the Austrian state created the Leopold Museum to house his collection and Leopold is employed as the director of the museum for life. Further, he is to receive additional substantial funds in the future. He is using his newfound wealth to buy more art. Once a collector, always a collector.

After years of searching and buying, Leon Dixon of Detroit owns one thousand Art Deco bicycles. His collection includes a 1936 Sears Bluebird worth $10,000 that retailed for $45.95 and a 1937 Firestone Super Streamline worth $6,000 that originally sold for $39.95.

Marshall Hahn, Jr., has collected contemporary self-taught art for thirty-five years. His collection, valued at $1 million, was given to the High Museum of Art, Atlanta.

Defying common wisdom, Barbara Jacobson started a collection of modern furniture. As it had been fifty years since this style was introduced, she reasoned that only the best had survived and that those pieces should be worth collecting. She is right, of course, as they become a part of our social and cultural history. Jacobson brings impeccable creditentials to her task, being an art historian and a trustee of the Museum of Modern Art in New York.

Stuart and Marilyn Kaplan have assembled one of the world's finest collections of playing cards and items related to them. Included in their collection are three thousand antique card games.

David Karpeles of Santa Barbara, California, a former professor and now a real estate investor, maintains five private museums to exhibit his one million documents and manuscripts. He started collecting at age forty-two, after being inspired by a visit to the Huntington Library in San Marino, California. A heavy buyer at auctions and through dealer catalogues, he is one of the outstanding collectors in the country.

Aaron Lansky collected Yiddish language material as no one else had before or since. His motivation was to renew interest in and the study of Yiddish. Through an imaginative network of fellow searchers he stimulated, over one million items were uncovered. Lansky formed the National Yiddish Book Center in Northhampton, Massachusetts, to house the works. He has distributed material to 150 institutions. The John D. and Catherine MacArthur Foundation was so impressed they awarded him a "genius grant" of $225,000.

On a chance visit to the Renwick Gallery in Washington, D.C., Jane and Arthur Mason became America's leading collectors of wood turnings—bowls and other designs handworked out of blocks of wood. The Masons were immediately attracted to the wood objects they saw in an exhibition at the gallery and set off on their own pilgrimage. They now own several hundred and have given many away, including several to the Renwick, as their way of saying thanks.

Walter Pforzheimer, a careerist with the Central Intelligence Agency, now has his own intelligence service library, second only to the CIA's library, which he started. The several thousand volumes in his "spy collection" are promised to his alma mater, Yale University. He keeps it under lock and key, of course.

Richard Knoph collects HO scale trains that are 100 percent accurate scale replicas. He has 250 train models including every train to run in America since 1900.

Charles Sebesta, of Texas, has collected 200,000 railroad nails. The oldest dates back to 1883. They come from 240 railroads in forty-nine states and eight countries. Sebasta issues a newsletter regularly. There are about five hundred "date-nail" collectors, and they meet twice a year. Among the interesting facts one learns from Sebesta are that the Germans used plastic nails during World War II, and Texas had 30 railroads. He estimates his collection is worth $100,000. Top value is $500 for a nail used on the Santa Fe Railroad.

Pierre Barinon, a Frenchman, collects Ferraris that have won famous races. He buys them directly from the winning race team. He has owned as many as fifty and has his own race track to run them on. His 312 PB, 450m hp, valued at $1 million, can hit 200 miles per hour. His 250 GT, which won the Tour de France race in 1961, is worth $1.5 million.

George Way collects Elizabethan and Jacobean furniture. He has never paid more than $2,500 for any one piece. His prize is a ten-foot-high Elizabethan oak canopy bed with carvings of Elizabeth I's initials and her coat of arms, now worth $400,000. Way works in a delicatessen and buys at flea markets and antique stores. He once bought a silver spoon for $20 at a local flea market, then saw a similar spoon on display at the Metropolitan Museum of Art: it was from the seventeenth century and worth $20,000. In a second-hand clothing store he found a landscape painting that had been painted by Hobbema, a well-known Dutch artist, valued in the hundreds of thousands of dollars.

Rick Edmissten, a Californian, collects old fishing lures. He owns more than 2,500 rods and reels worth $500,000. Edmissten is co-author of *Fishing Lure Collectibles* guidebook. His trophy is a six-inch copper minnow, 1859, worth $2,500. He buys at tackle shows, antique stores and flea markets as well as from other collectors, and plans to found a tackle museum.

Steven Michaan started collecting fish decoys a decade ago. He has assembled three hundred hand-carved bass, trout and perch. He paid $20 for his first decoy in 1985—a two hundred-year-old painted fish. By 1990, a 1920 glass-eyed trout was auctioned for $18,700 by Sotheby's. His decoys are now worth $2 million.

Phil Lobred, operator of a sports-fishing marina in San Diego, collects knives. He now has several hundred valued from $12 to $10,000. Today there are 100,000 collectors of knives who support an annual Custom Knife Show in New York, the Art Knife Collector Association in Winter Park, Florida, and at least three national magazines.

A surprising and winding tale starts with John Mulholland, a magician, friend of the famous Harry Houdini, and author, who assembled the world's finest collection of books and objects on magic. Upon his death, Mulholland's collection went to the Players Club in New York City, and then to auction at Swanns Galleries, where it was acquired by the head of a California bank that eventually went bankrupt (perhaps practicing some sleight of hand with deposits and loans). The federal government then took over and sold the Mulholland collection to Las Vegas magician David Copperfield for $2.2 million, about double what the defunct bank had paid. From what hat is it apt to appear next?

Philip Von Storch, a seventeenth-century German scholar, turned spy for England to further his collection of gems. He even stole from exhibitions.

William and Evelyn Thunell have been buying Hires Root Beer collectibles for thirty years, gathering two hundred items. Their most valuable piece may be a syrup dispenser, which they value at $50,000.

For years Mr. and Mrs. A. K. Miller lived on a Vermont farm without electricity or plumbing. When the widowed Mrs. Miller died, neighbors found $800,000 in hoarded gold under the floor boards. In the broken-down barns were forty-five classic automobiles. Christie's auctioned them off for a total of $2,200,000, including $173,000 for a 1920 Stutz Bearcat.

Charlotte H. Dinger became the world's leading collector and authority on antique carved horses and other carousel objects. She fell in love with the moving wooden horses as a child. Then by chance in 1972, while visiting an antique store, she found a carved horse for sale and thus started on a collecting effort that lasted the rest of her life. The first horse cost her $75. They now sell for as much as $175,000. Her best pieces are housed in the Carousel museum in Lahaske, Pennsylvania.

Max and Heidi Berry of Washington, D.C., collect in different areas including mechanical banks and toys—and almost anything that has a horse in or on it. They are both art and horse lovers.

Boston's Bertram Cohen began collecting marbles as an activity he could share with his son. His collection now includes marbles that date from the third century and one that weighs seventeen pounds.

Dr. Stanley Burns, a New York City eye surgeon, has a collection of 200,000 historic photographs. "I collect what other people throw away." Many museums want his collection, and television producers find his rare photographs a source of information.

The author of the James Bond novels, Ian Fleming, collected books that "made things happen." He included Darwin on evolution, Marie Curie on radium, Freud on the subconscious, Alexander Graham Bell on the telephone—a thousand books in all. Upon his death the collection went intact to the Lilly Library at Indiana University.

Thomas Jefferson Fitzpatrick, an early 1900s assistant professor at the University of Nebraska whose top salary was $1,800 a year, accumulated a library of ten thousand volumes on botany and related sciences. Every room in his house was filled from floor to near ceiling. His collection is now at the university. Collecting is not only for the wealthy.

Richard Gilder and Lewis E. Lehrman collect American historical manuscripts and now own the leading archive in private hands. It includes original material from Abraham Lincoln, George Washington and Benjamin Franklin as well as Gerald Ford's pardon of Richard Nixon.

The following anecdote demonstrates the friendships collecting can spawn. William Self, a California film and television producer, collects books by Charles Dickens. In this pursuit, he found himself often losing out at auctions to another collector, Kenyon Sterling, who consistently outbid him. Self determined to meet his nemesis and traced him to Dayton, Ohio, where, coincidentally, Self had been born and raised. Once the the two collectors met, they became close friends, traveling together and exchanging information and advice. After a while, Self noted that Sterling repeatedly advised him not to buy certain items. This puzzled Self because they were valuable and desirable, and he questioned Sterling as to why he was doing this. "Because I am going to will you my collection and I already have these." Once that happened, Self was in possession of the finest Dickens collection in private hands. Sterling, who collected subjects besides Dickens, left ten thousand volumes to his alma mater, Stanford University. Until then, Stanford had never heard from him.

Steven Guarnaccia of New Jersey, collects all sorts of things that children love—toys, games, puzzles, party favors, whistles, even promotional gizmos. Once a kid, always a kid.

Lawrence Scripps Wilkinson, a graduate engineer and retired executive of F.A.O. Schwartz, one of the finest of all toy stores, succumbed to his business interests and created a collection of American toys. It has grown so large and the quality is so high that it is now housed in the Detroit Historical Museum and has been exhibited at the Louvre in Paris and the Victoria and Albert Museum in London. It all started with a $100 purchase of a Lionel electric locomotive.

Not surprisingly, Barry Halper, a partner in the New York Yankees baseball club, collects baseball memorabilia. He owns one thousand uniforms, three thousand autographed baseballs, a million baseball cards and scores of historic programs. He plans to create his own traveling museum so sports fans over the country will have an opportunity to see these historical items.

Bill and Jan Schmidt, owners of a Coca-Cola bottling plant, are building in Elizabethtown, Kentucky, a new museum to be known as the Schmidt Museum of Coca-Cola Memorabilia. The 80,000-square-foot edifice will cost $25 million and be designed by the world-famous architect Frank Gehry.

Maxine Waters, a United States congresswoman from Los Angeles, collects black dolls. She bought her first doll in the 1960s and now has three hundred. Waters collects wherever her travels take her, including the Bahamas, where her husband, Sydney Williams, is the U.S. Ambassador.

Judi Hofer of Portland, Oregon, has collected two thousand dolls, including a limited edition of a 1914 Lord Fauntleroy worth about $20,000. She hopes to establish a museum to house her dolls.

The actress Demi Moore, of Los Angeles and Idaho, is partial to one-of-a-kind contemporary dolls from all over the world and probably has the largest collection. She, too, has plans to found her own doll museum.

Carole and Barry Kaye, Los Angeles, have opened a museum to house their collection of miniatures, all of which they have had made. It is considered the finest of its type in the world. They have one-inch-to-a-foot scale models of Hampton Court, Fontainebleau, the Doge's Palace and Chinese temples and have in progress the Vatican and Buckingham Palace. Auction houses regularly have sales of miniatures, which are over a $100 million business today. Miniatures have been around for centuries. The Pharaohs had miniature models of artifacts of daily life fashioned to help make their afterlife more comfortable. German royalty had the first doll houses made to instruct their children on housekeeping. In the 1920s Queen Mary, wife of King George V, was given a a miniature house that is now on display at Buckingham Palace. One of the most popular permanent exhibits at the Art Institute of Chicago is the world-famous Thorne miniature rooms created by Mrs. James Ward Thorne.

After discovering that his father's 1914 Stellite automobile was being used as chicken coop on their farm, B. Scott and June Isquick of Peper Pike, Ohio, began to collect vintage automobiles. They now own fourteen valuable cars. One never knows how a person may be enticed to become a collector.

Richard Hampton Jenrette lives in New York City but collects nineteenth-century houses. He owns six grand houses, which he has restored to their original status and style. He also collects American furniture from the same period so that he may properly furnish his houses.

Over a twenty-five-year period, John High, a former actor, accumulated thousands of postcards that illustrate and celebrate theatrical subjects. He has donated his collection to the Lake County Museum, Illinois, and endowed the collection with a $10,000 annual bequest.

Shirley and Lawrence Kalstone, New York City, have been collecting canes for twenty years, including a selection of gun canes that offer the user self-protection. Canes carved out of a single piece of wood are particularly valuable.

The painting that received the highest price ever paid—$82.5 million for Vincent Van Gogh's *Dr. Gachet*—was sold by Wynn Kramarsky of New York City. *Dr. Gachet* had been in the estate of his father, a banker from Holland who fled the Nazis and died in 1961. He still collects but never invests more than $5,000 a piece. Kramarsky has an exhibition space in New York and advises buyers on new and often unknown artists.

Richard and Pamela Kramlich, San Francisco, may be the only private video art collectors in the world. Their most expensive item is Bruce Nauman's *Raw Material—OK, OK, OK*, valued at $200,000.

Jay Leno, televison star, collects vintage motorcycles and bicycles. There are so many in his collection that he requires a separate building to house them.

The largest collection of Northwest Indian baskets in the country belongs to Alan Lobb of Seattle. He has been at it for thirty years and has published two books on the subject.

Peter Merolo, of New York, has a collection of animation art, heavily populated by Disney characters, including Snow White. A recent acquisition was Donald Duck and his three nephews.

Frank E. Grizzard, Jr., owns five hundred copies of John Bunyan's *The Pilgrim's Progress*. Four thousand editions have been published over three centuries.

Roger Phillips, a California architect, owns a ukulele collection and has become a skilled player. It started when he bought a ukulele kit for a friend for $3.95: once he had it assembled, he determined to learn to play it. He now performs at ukulele conventions. He claims that playing one "is like a dip in a pool on a hot day . . . very therapeutic."

One collection, that of Eli Broad, has benefited the American public in a particularly novel way. Broad, the founding chairman of the Los Angeles Museum of Contemporary Art, a contributor to education at his alma mater, Michigan State University, and a successful businessman, purchased a $2.5 million work of art on his American Express card and donated the 2.5 million airline miles he earned to students for travel.

The foremost collector of haute couture in the world, Sandy Schreier, Michigan, has ten thousand creations by fashion designers such as Balenciaga, Chanel, Fortuny, Poiret and Worth, most of which are of museum quality. She is particularly fascinated by Hollywood fashion.

Norma and William D. Roth, Florida, have the leading collection of headdresses and beadworks. They acquire items from over the world. Among their treasures is a Chinese crown decorated with gold, pearls, and furs.

Stephen Visakay, New Jersey, has an obsession for cocktail shakers and now has 1,200 sets worth $350,000. He believes he has about thirty fellow cocktail-shaker collectors in all, including James Thompson, the former Governor of Illinois.

Golf has spawned thousands of collectors—so many that the Golf Collectors Society numbers 3,500 members who attend regularly scheduled meetings and receive a quarterly publication. The United States Golf Association, golf's ruling body with hundreds of thousands of members, maintains the largest library of golf books in America at its headquarters in Far Hills, New Jersey. Virtually all the volumes were contributed by members or bought with funds provided by members.

Mark Zukerman of Carmel, Indiana, has assembled the largest collection of golf scorecards in the world—more than two thousand from that many different golf courses around the world. Mark says, "Golf scorecard collecting is a labor of love for me, nothing else." He runs his own business full time.

A retired insurance business owner in Boynton Beach, Florida, has become the leading authority on amateur golf. John Gleason has collected virtually everything ever published on the subject. He has a large research library containing reports on every United States amateur and Walker cup competition played. His goal is to publish the definitive book on amateur golf in America.

Ted Hoz, Baton Rouge, has been entered in the Guinness Book of World Records for collecting over 38,000 golf balls. To solve the storage problem, he has built cabinets that hold more than 7,000 balls each. Each ball is entered in his computer program so that he can locate them immediately.

Matty Reed, a retired Southern Pacific railroad engineer, has collected close to fifty thousand golf clubs and keeps them in his home in Fort Worth, Texas. He and his wife, Mildred, have been collecting for sixty-eight years. Their sons and grandchildren will have them all in time.

Louis I. Szathmary II, a Hungarian emigrant who came to America in 1951 with $1.10 in his pocket and fourteen books, has given the University of Chicago, the University of Iowa, Indiana University and other institutions thousands of books, rare pamphlets and five centuries of manuscripts, all on food preparation and cooking. He amassed his collection while owning and operating a restaurant in Chicago. The donations were his way of saying "thank you" for the opportunity America had given him.

Boyd Walker, retired professor, began collecting fetishes (miniature stone animals carved by the Zuni tribe) in the 1960s. His collection is now the single most comprehensive and best documented in the world. He has given the bulk of his 4,000 piece collection to the National History Museum of Los Angeles which at the time owned only two dozen. Margaret Hardin, curator of anthropology, stated, "Boyd Walker has done a remarkable thing. He has assured the Zuni fetish carvers of the late 20th century will have their proper place in history."

A retired Milwaukee County deputy sheriff, John Wilson, and his wife, Nancy, a retired supervisor in the public school system, have spent twenty-five years collecting paper money. They buy at currency auctions and shows. Their collection, now very valuable, includes money printed as early as 1690 in the colonies. It all started when Nancy, as a child, found a three-legged buffalo nickel which turned out to be worth $90. When she married John, he joined the chase.

Marion M. Weaver of Geneva, New York, collects drain tiles and has founded a museum to exhibit them. The collection includes tiles made of wood, cement, stone and glass. One is over three thousand years old. Another was made by World War II German war prisoners at a factory in Ohio and has a swastika scratched on it.

Particularly revealing of the broadening involvement of collectors are the number of museums that have been founded to preserve and exhibit objects that might be considered either to be too commonplace or to have such limited exposure that people would not be interested. Not true, as this list of subjects of established American museums illustrates.

Alphabet
American pianos
American quilts
Anthracite mining
Antique dolls
Antique outboard
Antique sewing
Apothecary
Apples
Assassinations
Barbed wire
Baseball
Basketball
Bathroom tissue
Beverage containers
Bird books
Bird eggs
Bird nests

Black heritage
Border Patrol
Botanical
Broadcasting
Butterflies
Canals
Candy
Carousels
Cars used in movies
Cartoon art
Cats
Cattlemen
Church history and art
Cigar collectibles
Circus
Clocks
Clowns
Coca-Cola

Coins
Combat aircraft
Comic books
Compacts
Computers
Cosmetology
Country doctors
Country music
Cowboy artists
Cowboys
Cowgirls
Cows
Crafts
Cuban
Dairy items
Dirigibles
Disneyana
Dog mushing
Dogs
Dolls
Drag racing
Drugstore collectibles
Dutch folk culture
Early trades and
　farm collectibles
Elephant collectibles
Fetishes
Figure skating
Fire fighters
Firearms
Firehouses
Fishermen
Fishing tackle
Flags
Florida's Army
Fly fishing

Football
Fossil beds
Fraternal organizations
Frogs
Funerals
Fur trade
Glass
Golf
Harness racing
Hollywood wax figures
Holocaust
Holography
Horses
Ice cream collectibles
Insulators
Iron and steel
Jails
Jazz
Jello
Keys
Kitchen collectibles
Kites
Knights of Columbus
Labels
Little Golden Books
Log cabins
Logging
Lumber
Marbles
Medical devices
Militaria
Milk bottles
Mining and industry
Model railroads
Money
Motors

Music boxes
Naval aviation
Newspapers
Neon art
Ocean liner collectibles
Padlocks
Paper clips
Paper dolls
Patriotic collectibles
Pencils
Petroleum
Phosphate
Pig collectibles
Pinball machines
Playing cards
Pocket knives
Police collectibles
Political items
Polo
Postcards
Pottery
Punch boards
Puppetry arts
Racing
Radio characters
Radios
Railroads
Robotics
Rock and roll
Norman Rockwell
Rodeos
Safaris
Salem witches
Satirical art
Scouting
Sewing items

Shells
Skiing
Slate shingles
Soda fountains
Softball
Soft drinks
Souvenir buildings
Space exploration
Spark plugs
Sports art
Submarines
Teapots
Teddy bear
Telephone pioneering
Telephony
Tennis
Texas Rangers
Thimbles
Tobacco art and history
Tools
Tow trucks
Toys
Toy trains
Trolley cars
War planes
Water mills
Western Americana
Whaling and whales
Whiskey bottles
Wooden boats
World's Fairs
World of records
World War I
World War II
Yachting
Zodiacs

101

Many of the areas of collectors' activity are supported by collectors clubs, which issue bulletins and newsletters and meet on occasion, some of them regularly. You will find nearly five hundred of them listed in Warman's *American and Collectibles Encyclopedia*. They are easy to join and will serve you well. Their numbers grow every year as collectors' interests continue to expand.

Chapter 10

Fascinating Characters – Paragons and Miscreants of The Collecting World

"The gathering of my books is the only thing I have accomplished in my life which gives me real satisfaction. Other than this, I have never regarded myself as other than a failure."

– Bernard Berenson

A SPECIAL JOY and attraction of being a collector is the fascinating, often unbelievable, characters you may come to know or learn about. Few activities are apt to draw as many or as interestingly unusual people pursuing their goals and dreams. Here are a few who have brought color and life and even controversy to collecting over the years.

One of the strangest characters to grace the international art scene was Bernard Berenson. A little fellow born of Latvian immigrant parents, Berenson was a Harvard graduate who ran away to Italy with a woman married to an Irish Catholic husband. When the husband died, Berenson, a Jew, converted to Catholicism and married the unfaithful lady. Berenson lived most of his life in Florence. A wily connoisseur, he became a legendary authority on Renaissance art, which he parlayed into a small fortune by authenticating paintings for dealers, principally Joseph Duveen and Wildenstein, so that they could sell the works. Berenson received a percentage of each sale plus a retainer. Some of his activities were so questionable that Kenneth Clark, director of Britain's National Gallery, viewed Berenson as "sitting atop of a mound of corruption." Upon his death at age ninety-two Berenson left his villa, collection and library to Harvard.

Lord Clark, wealthy, aloof, author and host of successful art programs on public television as well as director of the National Gallery, was himself somewhat eccentric. He had art dealer Lord Duveen rejected for reelection as a trustee after he had been voted a new term. He claimed that Duveen used his position as a trustee to advance his own interests. Clark appealed to then Prime Minister Neville Chamberlain to cancel the reappointment. Later, upon learning that Duveen was suffering from terminal cancer at the time (he died shortly thereafter), Clark admitted he should not have urged this action. Duveen had been the most generous of all of the trustees in gifting the National Gallery.

Armand Hammer was a mysterious, agent-like character whom no one really understood and to whom no one ever became close. He was a medical doctor who did not practice medicine; a friend of Russian communist leaders from Lenin to Gorbachev; a wheeler-dealer who could do business with a dictator like Kadafi of Libya, a man who made a fortune selling Russian art he had acquired at bargain-basement prices because of his contacts (he sold the Russian art through American department stores); a collector who set out to build a collection for himself, formed his own art gallery and then bought a second one so that he could acquire his art at lower prices; a would-be philanthropist who promised his entire collection to a major museum and then reneged and built his own museum with corporate funds. Fascinating!

Paul Sachs, an investment banker turned educator, developed at Harvard the first college or university program to teach "museumology." This was and still is the training ground for future museum curators and directors. A founding trustee of the Museum of Modern Art in New York as well, he had tremendous impact on the museum world as his graduates assumed top positions at the leading museums.

Dr. Franklin Murphy, like Sachs an educator who had great influence on the art world, graduated from medical school and then turned to education. He became head of two universities, the University of Kansas and then University of California at Los Angeles, where a sculpture garden was created in his honor. He served as a Trustee of the Los Angeles County Museum of Art, the J. Paul Getty Trust and the National Gallery, where he succeeded Paul Mellon as chairman. While a Trustee of the Getty, he was instrumental in employing Harold Williams as President. His acumen and wisdom qualified him as a most productive contributor to our museums and culture.

As director of the Museum of Fine Arts, Boston, Perry Rathbone recommended purchase of a Raphael portrait that had been imported illegally. It was a major catastrophe at the time for this marvelous museum. Rathbone was a graduate of Paul Sachs's course on "museumology" at Harvard and should have known better.

Gertrude Stein and her brother Leo spent most of their lives as expatriates living in Paris. They bought art from the many artists with whom they became friends. Gertrude wrote in a style and format that was never copied. Their home was a must-call for artists, writers and American collectors who lived in or visited Paris. In contrast to that of their close friends, the Cone sisters from Baltimore, the Steins' collection was dispersed over the world.

Mary Cassatt, artist and advisor, raised in Philadelphia, lived in Paris for most of her life and died there. She may have had a liaison with Edgar Degas for years, and another with James Stillman, a New York banker, who referred to "Mary Cassatt's million dollar advice." Recognized as one of America's outstanding artists, her paintings hang in the Metropolitan Museum, the National Gallery, the Art Institute of Chicago and many other major museums. Cassatt knew the French Impressionist artists and advised her collector friends to buy them. Mrs. Potter Palmer bought several Impressionist paintings on her advice and saw them grow greatly in value. Louisine Havemeyer, who became Cassatt's closest friend, gave her a car and chauffeur, which she used the rest of her life. Cassatt painted a portrait of Mrs. Havemeyer and her daughter. Durand-Ruel was her dealer. A recipient of the French Legion d'Honneur, her life came to a sad finish. She was stricken with blindness; Degas, her beloved brother and Stillman had all died, and she fell out with Mrs. Havemeyer. One of Cassatt's paintings sold for over $4 million in 1996, far more than she had earned in her entire lifetime.

Calouste Gulbenkian, an oil magnate and a prolific collector from the Middle East, lived the last ten years of his life in a hotel because he felt less lonely there. He was so secretive that few details of his private life are known. Stealthy, short, energetic, paranoiac, trusting no one, with commanding eyes like Morgan's, he traveled with both British and Turkish passports to his many residences. Gulbenkian maintained no office despite his worldwide business activities; he simply went to a nearby park with his secretaries and bodyguards. He kept his art collection in houses he owned in Paris, London, Lisbon and Washington, D.C., as well as selected museums. No one was allowed to enter any of his homes during this period, so much of his collection went unseen. His only explanation was, "Would I admit a stranger to my harem?"

Belle da Costa Greene was J. P. Morgan's secretary and chief assistant at his library for many years. Morgan had faith in her judgment and everyone had to clear Belle before being able to see the great man. Thus she knew almost all of the business, political and art leaders of that period and accumulated considerable power and influence. Morgan trusted her insight regarding art, as well. She became his librarian in 1905 at age twenty-one and remained in this position until his death in 1913. Morgan's son Jack named her director of the Pierpont Morgan Library in 1924, and she served in that capacity until retiring in 1948.

An employee of the Library of Congress, Howard Lamarr Walls broke into a long-overlooked and locked vault in 1942 and uncovered a treasure-house of forgotten original prints of the earliest movies made in this country. There were nearly four hundred works by D. W. Griffith and many of Mary Pickford's earliest movies as well as documentary footage of historic events such as the 1906 San Francisco earthquake. Walls was appointed a one-man staff to examine and care for these rare items, which he did for many years. The staff now numbers ninety and takes in about thirty thousand theatrical and television films a year. Walls, now retired in California, is recognized as the key figure in preserving our nation's film library.

Andrew Heiskel, chairman and chief executuive officer of Time, Inc., publisher of such magazines as *Time*, *Fortune* and *Life*, responded to Ronald Reagan's request and served as the first chairman of the newly created President's Committee for the Arts and Humanities. Its purpose was to stimulate private giving to the arts and the humanities. Under Heiskel's leadership, millions of dollars in private funds were contributed to many organizations and new ways to stimulate interest were developed.

Thomas Hoving is a man with many careers—park commissioner, editor, lecturer, art consultant and historian, publisher, author—and perhaps the most controversial director of a museum in modern times. During his decade as head of the Metropolitan Museum of Art, some of his actions have been questioned by others, but there is no doubt of his impact on the museum field as he threw open doors by establishing "blockbuster" exhibitions that enticed the public to visit museums in numbers never before seen.

The twenty-sixth president of the United States, Theodore Roosevelt, was commissioned by the Smithsonian Institution in

1909 to collect specimens of big game in Africa. With two hundred porters and staff members, the safari was one of the largest ever conducted. Four tons of salt were required for the preservation of animals' skins. Roosevelt shot many trophies, including nine lions, and wrote a book, *African Game Trails*, based on his adventures. If either the Smithsonian or the Rough Rider even contemplated such a mission today, he would be run out of town. Incidentally, taxidermy has benefited from new techniques and materials. It is far easier today to preserve and mount animals thanks to the use of urethane for the body and head forms. Trophies look better and last longer.

An Englishman who changed his name to his wife's maiden name when he moved to Los Angeles to enter the real estate business, Arthur Gilbert created a world-class collection of English gold and silverware acquired largely from impoverished British estates. After pledging his collection to a major American museum, he abruptly canceled the understanding and bequeathed the $200 million collection to his native country, Great Britain. This was such a stunning reversal—normally the flow of treasures has been from England to America—that the British government went to extensive efforts to satisfy Mr. Gilbert's demands and expectations. As we can see from this case, things are seldom "normal" in the collector's world. The very characteristics that may make a person a passionate collector can color his or her relationship with institutions.

Events may even drive one from glory to tragedy. Alexander Kelch, a Russain gold mining industrialist during the closing years of the reign of Nicholas II, shared the royal family's fascination with the creations of the masterful Russian jeweler Carl Fabergé. Kelch had Fabergé design seven of his famous Easter eggs for his collection. Each was equal in quality and design perfection to those created for the royal family. Now starts the soap opera. Kelch's wife, Barbara, left her husband, fled to Paris with the seven eggs and sold them in 1920. Her abandoned husband had a more difficult time: he was reduced to selling cigarettes on the streets and was arrested in 1930 by the Communist government for corresponding with his wife in Paris. Kelch was sentenced to hard labor in Siberia and presumably died there. This tale of woe emerged recently because one his Fabergé eggs was offered for sale at a Christie's auction.

Daniel Terra, son of Italian immigrants and a successful manufacturer, accumulated a fine collection of American art and then opened his own museum on Michigan Avenue, Chicago. Unabated, he then turned to Europe at President Reagan's urging to help educate Europeans on American art. He built a museum at Giverny, France, within walking distance of Monet's home and studio and housed a collection of Impressionist paintings done by American artists. Europeans' increased appreciation for American artists is largely due to Terra's efforts.

Not quite as laudable a collector was Charles Tyson Yerkes. He made at least three fortunes in the public transportation field; operated in and then fled in disgrace from Philadelphia, Chicago, New York and London; was sentenced to prison; married several times and kept countless mistresses. In an attempt to offset his deplorable reputation, he gave the University of Chicago its major observatory, which it still operates, and acquired a substantial art collection. Upon his death, his widow found his financial affairs in rank condition and herself without adequate funds, which led to an auction of his remaining assets. The sale was newsworthy enough to attract the Vanderbilts, Whitneys and Wideners. His art collection, including pictures by Rembrandt, Corot, Hals and Turner, was completely dispersed and Yerkes faded into history.

Judge Elbert H. Gary, who put together the U.S. Steel Corporation with J. P. Morgan and then built and ran their largest mill in Gary, Indiana (yes, the city was named for the judge), had his collections sold at auction in 1928 for the then-huge sum of $1,700,000 ($30 million today). He beat the Depression by one year. Equally astute was Jerome Kern, the great composer. He sold his book and music collection in 1928 as well for the

109

same amount—$1,700,000. Some are just smarter than others.

Sir Anthony Blunt, surveyor of the Royal Collection for the Queen of England, was the last word on artistic matters within the Royal family's many castles and priceless collections. He was also a spy for a foreign country prior to, during and after World War II. His betrayal was such a stunning revelation that the announcement was made by Prime Minister Margaret Thatcher herself. Where is the honor?

Charles Saatchi, an Iraqi immigrant to England, with his brother Maurice created from scratch the largest advertising agency in the world. It lasted only a short while before their empire collapsed and the brothers were forced out. In the process and before the collapse, Saatchi became enamored of contemporary art and accumulated a huge collection of six hundred works. He required warehouses to store them all. His purchases were so massive that he impacted the market and artists he became interested in had their prices zoom. At this writing the future of the collection and Saatchi's advertising career are still in question. Incidentally, he started his collecting habit as a child with Superman comics.

Amy Lowell, the prominent and eminent Boston lady who enjoyed her cigars, collected John Keats materials that are now housed in a special room in the Houghton Library at Harvard. The book dealer Dr. Rosenbach named her the greatest woman collector of her time.

Estelle Doheny, widow of the oil baron Edward, was the most generous supporter of the Archdiocese of Los Angeles, and as such gave the Church her outstanding library of rare books and manuscripts, largely religious in nature, and built a handsome memorial building in her late husband's name to house it. The only stipulation was that nothing could be sold for twenty-five years. In 1987, almost twenty-five years to the day after the donation and several years after Doheny's death, the Archdiocese had Christie's auction off the entire library. It became the largest book auction in history and brought the Church $37.4 million.

Certainly one of the most mysterious and intriguing souls to enter the book collecting world was Haven O'More. He appeared suddenly from nowhere and immediately made his presence felt. No one seemed to know him then, and even several years later no one was ever able to clearly and correctly identify his background, activities or financial wherewithal. What did become apparent was that he was knowledgeable about books, insisted on buying only the best and had ample funds. He was charming, handsomely attired and apparently well-educated and successful. Thus he was welcomed, even courted, by the leading dealers and auction houses. People who did get to know him on the surface speculated that he might be an actor, a philosopher, a poet, an architect and a war hero. He claimed to have been on General MacArthur's staff, to have earned three doctorate degrees and to be able to speak several languages. Then, as suddenly as he had entered the collecting scene, it was announced that Sotheby's would conduct an auction of his library, which was valued at $6 million. The reason for this abrupt reversal from buyer to seller became known through a lawsuit that was brought against him by the parents of a certain Michael Davis. It was charged that O'More had an unwelcomed influence over Davis that had led to Davis supplying over $10 million in funds that had been used by O'More to acquire the collection. Davis's parents prevailed, and the collection was ordered sold. O'More, despite showing much bravado during the auction, then disappeared as quickly as he had arrived. In the course of the trial it was revealed that none of the claims O'More had made regarding his past accomplishments was true. Oh, yes—the auction was a huge success.

Chapter 11

THE IMPORTANCE OF DEALERS – HOW TO DEAL WITH THE MIDDLEMEN

"I am particularly in debt to art dealers all over the world. I hear many of my colleagues say, 'I found this or that.' They usually neglect to say they discovered it at a dealer."

– William S. Lieberman, chairman of the Department of 20th Century Art, Metropolitan Museum of Art

"In the exhibitions they mount in their galleries, dealers provide an immensely important cultural service to the public. It is the dealers who show new art."

– Hilton Kramer, art critic and editor, *The New Criterion*

"What would have become of us if Kahnweiler had not had a good head for business?"

– Pablo Picasso

DEALERS HAVE LONG PLAYED an important role in assisting collectors. The first art dealer on record was Giovanni Battista della Palla in Florence, Italy, in the sixteenth century. He worked for the Medici familiy as they assembled the greatest art collection on the continent.

The dealer's main function is to serve collectors, many of whom do not have the time to develop the knowledge or connections necessary. The reputable dealer expends time, energy and

The Importance of Dealers

money in searching for artistic material, investigates the authenticity of objects and their provenance and restores objects when necessary. Dealers also maintain their own inventory, otherwise they would have nothing to sell; thus dealers are large buyers as well as sellers. The dealer takes risks, as do all business people, and is entitled to a fair profit for his or her efforts and skills. A dealer may serve you as an advisor, if you so choose. Art dealers tend to represent certain kinds of styles, periods or artists–or example, contemporary, Renaissance, American, Impressionist and so forth. Dealers who specialize in areas other than art, such as coins, stamps, antique automobiles and books, are similarly experienced, adept and helpful.

Dealers can be a vital part of the collector's life and activity. It is important that the collector become familiar with dealers he or she may turn to for guidance and acquisitions. Here are a few simple steps that will be helpful to this process: Ask dealers to show you their slide files, which contain other works of the artists they represent. Ask to see their press book, which should carry coverage of their artists. These will give the collector an overview of the work and the sources available. Dealers are usually pleased to do so. Obtain the names of a few key clients. Ascertain that the dealer is in the position to convey good and full title to any object you buy.

Museums have found it profitable to cooperate with dealers. Dealers know where the fine objects in private collections are and may be of help in obtaining them for loans, or they may own fine objects themselves and often will make them available for exhibitions. Dealers frequently give money and objects to museums.

Dealers are organized into associations; you may call or write any of them and receive complete details regarding their members. In all, there a five and a half pages of art dealers and galleries listed in the Manhattan Yellow Pages, which gives an idea of how many sources are available to serve. Contact the dealer associations and/or your museum for references. You will find similar dealer listings in many other areas such as coins, stamps, books, manuscripts, autographs—indeed in practically any subject in which you may be interested.

Reputable dealers are capable of appraising your collection for insurance and tax purposes. They can locate objects for you and assist you in their acquisition. As recently as 1997 a pair of New York dealers arranged for the acquisition of a major painting by Cézanne by a New York collector for $50 million. It was acquired from a French dealer who had arranged for the necessary export license. A transaction done in this manner is usually totally secretive until completed. This sale was reported as a major news story by the *Wall Street Journal*.

Dealers who operated in the past, some of whose firms no longer exist, made many contributions in the nineteenth and early twentieth centuries. Being familiar with them will help the present-day collector understand the traditions and practices of this specialized field. These were talented people who pioneered this service. They worked with the great collectors at a time when hundreds of foreign treasures came to America.

Paul Durand-Ruel, son of the agency's founder, became the most important dealer to the French Impressionist artists and was most responsible for the acceptance of this new artistic expression. He supported the artists emotionally and financially, buying paintings from them when they needed money. He purchased Rousseau's entire studio at one time, bought twenty-three pictures from Monet on another occasion. He was the first dealer to export Impressionist paintings to America. He pioneered exhibitions in France and the United States of Impressionist artists and opened an office in New York in 1887. In this fashion he enticed H. O. Havemeyer into purchasing forty Impressionist pictures at one time, most of which ended up in the Metropolitan Museum. Over many years Durand-Ruel represented Cassatt, Degas, Delacroix, Millet, Monet, Pissarro, Rousseau, Gauguin, Manet, Sisley and Renoir, who painted his portrait. During a fifty-year period nearly every masterpiece of French paintings passed

The Collectors

Henry Edwards Huntington, 1907. Courtesy of the Huntington Library.

Pierpont Morgan, 1902. Courtesy of the Archives, The Pierpont Morgan Library, New York.

Charles L. Hutchinson, president of The Art Institute of Chicago's Board of Trustees (1882-1924), first page from Hutchinson's scrapbook, c. 1924. Courtesy of Mr. and Mrs. Carl T. Schuneman, Jr. Photograph © 1998, The Art Institute of Chicago. All Rights Reserved.

Martin Ryerson, 1904. Photograph © 1998, The Art Institute of Chicago. All Rights Reserved.

In Praise of America's Collectors

Sir Oswald Hornby Joseph Birley, *Andrew W. Mellon*, 1933, oil on canvas. Gift of Mrs. Mellon Bruce, National Gallery of Art, Washington. © Board of Trustees, National Gallery of Art, Washington.

William F. Draper. *Paul Mellon*, 1974, oil on canvas. Paul Mellon Collection, National Gallery of Art, Washington. © Board of Trustees, National Gallery of Art, Washington.

Henry Clay Frick. © The Frick Collection, New York.

John Singer Sargent, *Isabella Stewart Gardner*, 1888, oil on canvas. © Isabella Stewart Gardner Museum, Boston.

The Importance of Dealers

Samuel H. Kress, early 1900s. Courtesy of the Samuel H. Kress Foundation.

Sir Joseph Duveen. National Portrait Gallery, Smithsonian Institution.

Mr. J. Paul Getty and his dogs at Sutton Place in England. Courtesy of the J. Paul Getty Trust.

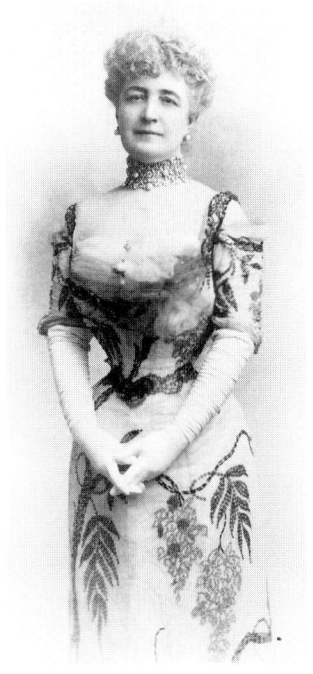

Mrs. Potter Palmer, 1900. Photograph ©1998, The Art Institute of Chicago. All Rights Reserved.

In Praise of America's Collectors

Franklin D. Roosevelt, 1938 (?). Courtesy of the Franklin D. Roosevelt Library.

Arthur A. Schomburg, Courtesy of the Arthur A. Schomburg Photograph Collection, The New York Public Library.

Edward Steichen, *Portrait of Gertrude Vanderbilt Whitney*, 1937, gelatin silver print. Collection of Whitney Museum of American Art, Gift of the family of Edith and Lloyd Goodrich. © 1997 Whitney Museum of American Art.

Lillie P. Bliss, 1927. Courtesy of The Museum of Modern Art, New York.

The Importance of Dealers

John D. Rockefeller, Jr., 1933.
Courtesy of the Rockefeller Archive Center.

Charles L. Blockson. Courtesy of the Charles L. Blockson Afro-American Collection.

Peggy Guggenheim, c. 1942. © The Solomon R. Guggenheim Foundation, New York.

Wilhelmina Cole Holladay, founder and chairman of the board, the National Museum of Women in the Arts. Courtesy of the National Museum of Women in the Arts.

In Praise of America's Collectors

"AMERICA'S CATHEDRALS ARE HER MUSEUMS."
– André Malraux

The Art Institute of Chicago, view of Michigan Avenue entrance looking southwest, 1990. Photograph © 1998, The Art Institute of Chicago. All Rights Reserved.

The Metropolitan Museum of Art, Fifth Avenue facade, 1970. Courtesy of the Metropolitan Museum of Art.

The Importance of Dealers

California Palace of the Legion of Honor. Courtesy of the California Palace of the Legion of Honor, Fine Arts Museums of San Francisco.

East Building of the National Gallery of Art, Washington, opened 1978, I.M. Pei, architect. © Board of Trustees, National Gallery of Art, Washington.

Library Exhibition Hall, The Huntington Library, Art Collections, and Botanical Gardens, San Marino, California. Courtesy of the Huntington Library.

In Praise of America's Collectors

The Solomon R. Guggenheim Museum. © The Solomon R. Guggenheim Foundation, New York.

San Francisco Museum of Modern Art's new building exterior, 1994. Courtesy of SFMOMA.

The Getty Museum's entrance facade, seen from the tram arrival plaza at the Getty Center, opened 1997, Richard Meier, architect. Courtesy of the J. Paul Getty Trust.

through Durand-Ruel's hands. He provides an excellent example of a dealer helping to support artists and being the window to bringing new, fresh artistic ideas to market. Durand-Ruel was awarded the Legion d'honneur by a grateful French government. When being applauded for his many contributions, Durand-Ruel replied, "Don't congratulate me. We dealers have to thank the collectors."

Wildenstein and Company is an international French dealer still very active and now managed by the fourth generation. An office was opened in New York 1901 and the company now operates in London and South America as well as Paris. Wildenstein deals in a wide range of artists, including Rembrandt, Rubens, Vermeer, Renoir, El Greco, Goya, Fragonard, Cézanne, Monet, Degas, Gauguin and Van Gogh. The firm built up its "stock" by buying complete collections and pursuing great objects. It maintains a library of 300,000 volumes as well as more than 100,000 photographs and catalogues and also publishes scholarly catalogues of artists and their works. After splitting with Duveen, Bernard Berenson collaborated with the firm.

In 1846 Knoedler and Company became the first European dealer to open in New York (by the early 1900s all the large international dealers were there). Among its clients were the Vanderbilts, Henry Flagler, Leland Stanford, Jay Gould and Andrew Mellon. The Knoedler firm was purchased by Armand Hammer in 1972.

Dr. A. S. W. Rosenbach, who lived and worked in Philadelphia, was the twentieth century's best known rare book dealer. His clients included J. P. Morgan, H. E. Huntington, Lessing Rosenwald, and the Widener family, with whom he worked closely to assemble the collection that went to Harvard and is now housed in the Widener Library. He bought as heavily as he sold and upon his death founded the Rosenbach museum and library in Philadelphia.

Jacques Seligmann, J. P. Morgan's number one dealer, started out by working at the Hôtel Drouot, which was a flea-market type of auction house in late-nineteenth-century Paris. His son Germain followed his father in the business (changing the spelling of his last name to a single "n"). They sold tapestries, sculpture, porcelains, ivories, enamels, marble figures and silver as well as pictures. Some of their clients, in addition to Morgan, were Benjamin Altman, Otto Kahn, Mrs. George Widener, Arabella Huntington, George Blumenthal. Seligmann, at Morgan's request, supervised the shipment of Morgan's art from London to New York when the duty for antiquities was removed. (The tariff laws were changed in 1910 so that any art one hundred years old or older was not subject to duty. That is when Morgan decided to bring all of his European art purchases home.) It took one year to ship his collection; on Janunary 29, 1913, the last of 351 cases was packed and sent to the Metropolitan Museum. Ironically, Morgan died in Rome on March 31, 1913, so he never saw his collections gathered together for exhibition in one place. At the time of his death, his collections were estimated to include more than 4,100 objects. Seligmann won Morgan's confidence by giving great service and a determination to prove the authenticity of every piece. Morgan grew to trust him implicitly. Seligmann was always prepared—he knew the object, educated the buyer, was confident, articulate, precise and dependable.

Thomas Agnew and Son, established in London in 1817, also worked closely with Morgan, as well as with J. Paul Getty and the Wideners. They helped Mr. and Mrs. Paul Mellon acquire their remarkable collection of English art that is now in the Yale Center for British Art.

Ambrose Vollard (1865-1939) specialized in Impressionist and Post-Impressionist art. His clients included the Havemeyers, Albert Barnes, even Monet. He handled Cézanne, Matisse, Van Gogh, and Picasso, giving the latter his first one-man show in Paris in 1901. His memoirs give fascinating insight into this period in Paris. Both Cézanne and Picasso painted Vollard's portrait.

Daniel-Henri Kahnweiler, a German who became a Parisian art dealer before World War I, specialized in Cubist art. He represented Juan Gris, Braque, Derain and Picasso, who painted his portrait, and advised artists on business matters as well. Kahnweiler lived in Switzerland during the war and upon his return to Paris found his entire estate had been seized by the French government under a war reparations act passed against all German citizens. After the war he entered into an exclusive contract to represent Picasso, published a biography of Juan Gris and lectured at leading universities.

Another fascinating character was René Gimpel, an in-law of Lord Joseph Duveen. Gimpel kept a diary that reveals much about the art world of his time. His clients included Altman and the Vanderbilts and Wideners. He remained in France during World War II, where he was active in the resistance movement; he was later captured and died in a German concentration camp.

Pierre Matisse, son of the great artist Henri, operated out of New York. Upon his death, his estate was purchased in 1990 by the American dealer William Acquavella in partnership with Sotheby's for $142.8 million. It included 2,300 works by Chagall, Miró, Giacometti, Dubuffet, Tanguy and others.

One dealer whose name keeps appearing in these pages was so influential and colorful a character that he merits his own section. The story of the life and times of Lord Joseph Duveen follows in Chapter 12.

Chapter 12

LORD JOSEPH DUVEEN – THE "BABE RUTH" OF ART DEALERS

"Lord Duveen was genuinely a great giver. His generosity was part of his whole expansive personality. How many art dealers have presented pictures or whole art galleries to the Nation? Scarcely one."
– Kenneth Clark, director of the National Gallery, London

"Duveen was the greatest salesman of his time."
– Sir Osbert Stillwell

THE CAREER OF LORD JOSEPH DUVEEN provides excitement, amazement and an historical perspective on what a dealer can and will do to serve a collector. Duveen was extravagant, bombastic, daring, dramatic, persuasive, generous and very successful. He dealt with the most dedicated, prolific and recognized collectors of the first forty years of the twentieth century and educated many of them. His efforts led to hundreds of the world's greatest treasures leaving Europe and taking up permanent residence in the private collections and museums in America. Works of art that Duveen acquired and then sold to American collectors now populate all the leading American museums. He was the single most influential dealer in the formation of the National Gallery in Washington, D.C., and in doing so shaped the art taste of Americans. As one historian observed, he lived among his fellow dealers and millionaire American collector clients, "like a member of British aristocracy, and rightly so, for among all dealers only Duveen was enobled." For these reasons, you may find this brief biographical sketch of interest and value.

Joseph Duveen came from an English family of art dealers and inherited the business at the turn of the twentieth century. At that time the firm specialized in porcelains, other decorative arts, tapestries and sculpture. Duveen moved it into the picture business and enlarged its premises and position in New York and Paris as well as London. Before his death in 1939, he had been knighted by King George V for his many acts of beneficence. Lord Duveen had donated many works of art to the Tate Gallery in England, including some by Cézanne, Gauguin, Hogarth and Sargent. He also gave the Tate a new wing for modern paintings and sculpture, a gallery wing to British Museum to house the Elgin marbles, an additional wing to the National Portrait Gallery and a wing for Venetian art to London's National Gallery, of which he was a trustee. He not only furnished the building funds for these new wings but also took charge of their design and followed every detail of their construction. In addition to his generosity in his native land, Duveen gave at least twenty paintings to various French museums and was justly honored by the French government.

Duveen sold paintings and other works of art to J. P. Morgan, Andrew Mellon, Samuel H. Kress, the Rockefellers, Benjamin Altman, P. A. B. Widener, Henry and Arabella Huntington (the Huntington Collection was supplied almost entirely by Duveen; Henry and Arabella bought $21 million worth of art and furniture from Duveen from 1908 to 1927), Henry Clay Frick, Philip Lehman and son Robert Lehman, Edward D. Libbey, Edward S. Harkness, John Ringling, the Rothschilds, Norton Simon, Mr. and Mrs. William Randolph Hearst, Mrs. Horace

Dodge, William C. Whitney, E. T. Stotesbury, Andrew Carnegie, Jules Bache, Henry Goldman (Goldman, Sachs), and many members of English and European royal families. Fifty-five of the 115 pictures Andrew Mellon gave to National Gallery were purchased from Duveen, as was almost half of Samuel Kress's collection, also donated to the National Gallery.

He did most anything and everything for his clients, including helping them design, build and furnish their great houses appropriately. He arranged the wedding of Arabella Huntington to her nephew, Henry E. Huntington, after her first husband, Colis, had died. He furnished the Detroit and Palm Beach homes of Mrs. Horace E. Dodge and the Philadelphia and Palm Beach homes of Mrs. E. T. Stotesbury. He arranged for Henry and Arabella Huntington to flee France in World War I when the Germans were within fifty miles of Paris. Henry Clay Frick's house on Fifth Avenue St. was designed by an architect Duveen chose. Duveen designed the Fragonard Room around eleven panels he had sold Frick and the Boucher Room around eight panels commissioned by Madame de Pompadour. The Frick Mansion became the site of the Frick Collection upon the death of Mrs. Frick in 1931.

J. P. Morgan asked Duveen to furnish his two London residences with the finest eighteenth-century French furniture and art available. (This was after Morgan had tested Duveen by asking him to identify the authentic pieces among the five Chinese jars he had placed on a table. Duveen promptly shattered the two fakes with his cane. Morgan was impressed.) While Duveen undoubtedly made a handsome profit he also performed a very important service for a man who was too busy to see to it himself.

Morgan's and the others' reliance on Duveen to furnish their homes demonstrates the trust that existed between client and dealer. Duveen often extended credit to his good clients and would help them out should they get in financial straits by buying back some or all of the objects he had sold them earlier. When Jules Bache's fortune vanished in 1929, he owed Duveen $4 million. With Bache's consent, Duveen took the art back and held it in reserve for him until his fortune was replenished. When Bache had improved his financial position, his art objects were returned to him by Duveen. Bache eventually gave his collection to the Metropolitan Museum. Duveen performed other services as well. At one time, J. P. Morgan inadvertently became entangled in a questionable art acquisition that eventually involved the French government. He asked Duveen to handle it for him and see that no one was embarrassed or accused of misdeeds. Duveen suggested that Morgan give one of the questioned works of art to the Louvre, which he did. The French government then conferred on Morgan the Grand Croix of the Legion d'honneur and closed the case. Everyone was pleased.

Artists he collected and sold included Rembrandt Van Rijn, Thomas Gainsborough, Jan Vermeer, Raphael, Frans Hals, Joshua Reynolds, George Romney, J. M. W. Turner, Jean-Honoré Fragonard, Jean Antoine Watteau, Anthony van Dyck, Peter Paul Rubens, Albrecht Dürer, Giovanni Bellini, Giovanni di Benvenuto, Sandro Botticelli, Correggio, Leonardo da Vinci, Tintoretto, Titian, Francisco de Goya, Diego Velázquez, Benvenuto Cellini, Donatello, Jean-Antoine Houdon and Giorgione. He held some works of art he bought for as long as four decades before selling them. He often bought entire collections for lump sums: that way no one but Duveen could attach a value to a specific work of art. In 1920, when the Huntingtons had decided to close their New York City mansion and move permanently to California, Duveen willingly repurchased all the objects they were not taking to California. Huntington was very grateful, of course. Six years later, Duveen took a freight car loaded with art to California. The Huntingtons bought the entire contents.

Duveen sold his collections for many times what he had paid for them. He purchased the famous Kann Collection early in the 1900s for $4.5 million. Shortly thereafter he sold to J. P. Morgan, Benjamin Altman and Arabella Huntington a very small portion of the total collection of paintings, sculptures and fine furniture for over $4 million. Thus he had quickly recovered almost all his purchase price and still owned over 80 percent of the collection. As another example, he sold to J. P. Morgan for $500,000 a tapestry for which he had paid $60,000 a few years previously.

On the other hand, no dealer matched Duveen's accomplishments or generosity. He is among a handful of people most responsible for bringing great art to the American people. He worked with and helped inspire the leading American collectors of the twentieth century. He brought works by the best European artists to America. The paintings, sculpture, tapestries, and furniture he sold represent some of the finest works of art in the collections of our greatest museums. No one can match his record.

He never employed sales people in the normal sense. He did have on his staff a rather shady character named Bertram Boggis who performed various services for Duveen and his clients that some thought might have been a little flagrant. Neither did Duveen advertise: he never even put a painting in one of his gallery windows. However, he went to great lengths to influence and motivate people to serve his purposes. He took care of the art critic of the London *Daily Telegraph* with cigars, clothing and other presents. The staff of many of his clients became beholden to Duveen because of the large gifts that he gave them, and they in turn told him many confidential things about their employers. These were some of the matters Boggis handled. Duveen housed his works of art in elegant, even majestic galleries. He called his Paris gallery his "Little Palace." It contained a grand staircase, marble courtyard and beautiful gardens. When J. P. Morgan paid his first visit, he admired it so much he offered to buy it from Duveen for his bank's Paris office. Duveen had a smaller version, five stories tall with thirty rooms, of the Ministry of Marine in Paris constructed especially for his gallery on Fifth Avenue in New York City. It was obviously an appropriate setting to view the world's greatest art. As few as a hundred buyers might visit the gallery in a year, but they were the cream of America's collectors. (Duveen was quite selective, and there were many to whom he would not sell.) One never left Duveen's under-impressed.

Duveen's sales pitch was classic: "Do you realize that the only thing you can spend $100,000 on without incurring an obligation to spend a great deal more for its upkeep is a picture? You can make more money, but if you miss this picture, you'll never get another like it. It is unique. Great paintings, unlike money, are difficult to acquire. It's easy to buy a $50,000 painting. It is difficult to get one that costs $250,000."

Duveen sold immortality. He frequently bought art or complete collections back from his clients when they died. For example, he repurchased from the estate of J. P. Morgan upon his death his entire porcelain collection—and then resold it to three of his favorite clients. Its value was enhanced by the fact that it had been owned by Morgan. He sold collections, not just a picture or a single work of art. He advised his clients, "Don't scatter. Concentrate." He created handsomely produced catalogues and books around his clients' collections. They paid for them, of course.

Mrs. William Randolph Hearst described Duveen as "a gentleman salesman in a cutaway. He met with everything he had. The fact is that you could not buy anything from Duveen. Everything was on reserve or promised to some one else. He didn't want to sell his stuff. They always badgered the poor fellow until he gave in." And Belle da Costa Greene, J. P. Morgan's librarian, after viewing a house Duveen had just furnished for a client, exclaimed: "It's so Duveen."

Duveen's most effective and longest-lasting professional association was with Bernard Berenson, scholar, author, world-recognized expert on Italian paintings and expatriate. Duveen made a secret deal with Berenson in the early 1900s. Berenson was to authenticate Italian paintings for Duveen and advise him as to which pictures he considered worth buying. The arrangement lasted thirty years, until 1938, when Berenson refused to authenticate the painting *Adoration of the Shepherds* as a Giorgione rather than a Titian. Duveen was selling it to Mellon, but when Berenson said it was a Titian, Mellon returned it. That was the end of the arrangement between dealer and scholar. Duveen later sold the same painting to Samuel Kress, and it is now in the National Gallery as a Giorgione. Strangely enough, Berenson then made a deal with George Wildenstein to perform for him the same service that he had done for decades for Duveen. Stranger still, Berenson later did attribute the painting to Giorgione, which was how Duveen positioned it originally. In his autobiography, Berenson wrote, "I took a wrong turn when I swerved from purely intellectual pusuits. The spiritual loss was great." A very sad finish to a life. Berenson made a profit on all the sales that Duveen made with his authentication. His commissions ran from 10 percent to 25 percent. This income allowed him to buy and maintain his estate and staff.

The impact of the Duveen-Berenson arrangement can be testified to by the fact that of 103 Italian pictures that Duveen sold during their thirty years partnership, 93 are now housed in museums, mostly American, 6 are still owned by known individuals and the locations of the remaining 4 are unknown. The great beneficiaries were the American public and their museums.

In 1936, when Andrew Mellon was spending a great deal of time in Washington, D.C., Duveen arranged to lease an apartment directly below Mellon's and filled it with forty-two works of art. He gave Mellon the key to apartment and invited him to visit it any time he chose. In about a year, Mellon purchased everything in the apartment. It was the largest single purchase of art in history at that time, valued at $21 million. All the works ended up in the National Gallery.

Samuel H. Kress became Duveen's largest client upon Mellon's death the next year. Most of his purchases from Duveen came in the last two years of Duveen's life. He actually ended up outspending Mellon. Duveen had helped make him interested in contributing art to the National Gallery as well. Since Mellon's name was not used in connection with the National Gallery, even though he had built it and had given all of his art to it, Kress, Chester Dale and Joseph E. Widener, also Duveen clients, all felt relaxed about giving their art to the people as well.

Duveen fakes, unintentional, did creep in on occasion. Two Vermeers from the Mellon Collection in the National Gallery were declared unauthentic several years later. They were *The Smiling Girl* and *The Lace Maker*. Others also disqualified (seventeen in all) included *Old Woman Plucking a Fowl*, previously attributed to Rembrandt; *George IV as the Prince of Wales*, thought to be by Gainsborough; and *Feast of the Gods,* sold as a Daumier. They had been given to the National Gallery by Lessing J. Rosenwald in 1943.

Not everyone was a great admirer of Lord Duveen. Ironically, even though he had been partially responsible for having Kenneth Clark named director of the National Gallery, of which Duveen was then a trustee, in 1937, solely on Clark's recommendation to the then Prime Minister Neville Chamberlain, Duveen was replaced as a trustee. He was at the time suffering with terminal cancer (he was to die in two years), and this crushed him. Later Clark noted that if he had known Duveen was so ill, he would not have pressed the issue.

Paul Mellon, son of Duveen's number one client for years, was also not fond of the dealer. He said, "I regard Duveen with distaste and thought him an impossibly bumptious and opinionated ass. I have never been able to understand how my father should have fallen under his spell, although one must bear in mind that Duveen had made himself one of the very few sources of fine pictures." Some art historians have gone even further, describing Duveen's operations as sordid, accusing him and Berenson of having practiced chicanery and even calling him a crook.

When Lord Duveen died in 1939 in his suite at Claridges Hotel in London, he had several million dollars in cash and art in his inventory and no debt—and this was after he had given away over $10 million to the National Gallery, the Tate Gallery and the British Museum.

In his will, Duveen left the firm to his key employees and handsome annuities to other employees. The art inventory "in the basement" generated $40 million in sales before the employee-owners sold out to Norton Simon in 1964. There was still a large inventory. Simon acquired not only the inventory but copious correspondence and documents that taught him much about the relationship between collector and dealer and the importance of research; as a result of the lessons he learned from Duveen, he became one of the world's most astute purchasers.

An art historian once called Duveen "the Babe Ruth of the art dealer's game." Knowing of the contradictory views of him hosted by his clients on the one hand, and by Paul Mellon, Bernard Berenson and Kenneth Clark on the other, one is reminded of the age-old saying, "Facts are precious. Opinions are less so." But no matter what controversies surrounded his life, no one can dispute that, all in all, Lord Joseph Duveen was a fabulous character whose impact on American museums will last forever.

Chapter 13

The Value of the Auction House – How to Buy at Auctions Wisely and Without Fear

---

"As is fitting in a democracy, auctions are open to all, and the only rules are the basic laws of economics."
– Douglas Dillon, former chairman of
the Metropolitan Museum of Art

AUCTIONS HAVE BEEN TAKING PLACE almost since the beginning of recorded history. In ancient Rome, in order to help finance a war he was waging, Marcus Aurelius sold at auction jewelry, vases, tapestries, and statuary that had belonged to Emperor Hadrian. He even included gowns that had been owned by the empress. In more modern times, auction houses have been providing an essential service for the last three centuries so well that their volume, profits and influence have grown tremendously. One of today's major houses, Christie's, held its first auction in 1766.

The auction market is the most liquid. Auction houses work on a commission received from both buyer and seller. They do not own the pieces that they are selling but exhibit the objects before the auction so that potential buyers may view them up close as they study the catalogue for the sale. Auctions give the seller broad national and international coverage, which enlarges the market. Auction houses see to it that the seller gets paid since they collect the sale price and keep the objects until checks, money orders and so forth have cleared. Thus the seller takes no risk of checks bouncing, false bank accounts or stolen credit cards.

Everyone at an auction has the same chance to acquire any object for sale, unlike at some galleries, where dealers buy for private clients, or at a flea market, where buyers are limited to those who happen by. A buyer may participate in an auction without actually being present by speaking by phone to a representative while the auction is going on and by submitting written bids prior to the auction. Children may participate under their parents' guidance, which can be a memorable learning lesson.

The major auction houses, when the property is substantial enough, will hold house auctions. In these instances the home of the owner is opened to the public, who may observe the objects to be sold in their appropriate setting. The auction is then held at the house. It's like an elegant garage sale. This took place with the legendary Pamela Harriman's estate. Following her death, Sotheby's was commissioned to sell the entire contents of her homes in Georgetown, Middleburg (Virginia), and Paris, where she was our ambassador. The sale, including art, silver, crystal, furniture and her collection of snuff boxes, garnered $8.7 million.

Auction houses now provide guarantees as to authenticity of objects they sell—except for drawings and paintings prior to 1870. Should you purchase at auction a painting or drawing dated before 1870, you have no recourse if the work turns out differently than labeled.

Sometimes auction houses issue a catalogue in which the terms of the sale are included. There is usually a charge for the catalogues, but they are worth it. The catalogue should carry all vital information on each object listed. The houses guarantee whatever is written in their catalogue. Study it carefully, and should you have any questions, ask them before the auction. The

The Value of the Auction House

major houses do an excellent job of researching objects before they are accepted and listed for sale. If you have the time, it is a smart practice to visit the auction house prior to the auction: the viewing period allows you to study the objects you are interested in before you make a bid. The times for the viewing periods are listed in the catalogue.

As the number of collectors has grown and the assortment of objects in which they are interested has increased, the auction houses have expanded to cover a wider range of collectibles. Christie's and Sotheby's are now auctioning lower-priced items. They hold classes on auctions, including mock auctions for those who have never attended one before or may not be sure as to procedures. Houses are becoming much more user-friendly. You can even earn airline mileage points. Auction houses now sell almost anything people collect. Sales of objects owned by famous people have skyrocketed. The results of the Jackie Kennedy Onassis auction were unbelievable. The George Burns auction was another example. Now the estates of Debbie Reynolds, Maximillian Schell, Benny Goodman, Claudette Colbert, Ginger Rogers, Lana Turner, Eva Gabor and Dinah Shore are all selling items at auction. There is no shame in auctioning off one's treasures—the stigma of selling has vanished. In 1997, just months before her death, Christie's auctioned off for charity seventy-nine gowns owned by Diana, the Princess of Wales, for over $3 million. The catalogues for the auction sold for $60 soft cover and $265 hard cover and raised another $1.5 million. The top bid was $222,500 for a gown she wore when dancing with John Travolta; it was purchased by a secret admirer. At a previous auction, the white suit Travolta wore in the film *Saturday Night Fever* went for $145,000. The auction business has grown so much that now the two largest houses are publicly traded, one listed on the New York Stock Exchange and the other in England. You can buy shares of stock in Sotheby's and Christie's if you so desire.

Auction houses will appraise your objects, usually free of

charge. You may call for an appointment or send photographs with pertinent information. Some hold "open houses" when anyone may bring in objects for appraisal. These are done on their premises or in conjunction with a local museum. A few houses have traveling appraisers who may appear in your community from time to time. They usually place a small advertisement in the local paper announcing dates, times and places. Auction houses are willing to provide this free service because they have found that frequently owners will consign their objects to the house for sale. This is a way to stimulate business.

The leading auction houses handle the more important objects and do not offer as wide a range of collectibles as some others do. The same is true of the major shows and dealers. That is why the three to four thousand independent exhibitions and sales are attractive to collectors. You will find them advertised or noted in local publications. The more important ones are apt to be listed in publications that go to people interested in collecting, such as art magazines and other specialized publications. They represent a large and growing market.

There are many specialty auction sales not conducted through the established auction houses. Hundreds of estate sales, antique exhibitions and other auctions are held every year. Just like the auction houses, they will all welcome you.

Chapter 14

FAKES, FORGERIES, STOLEN GOODS, COPIES AND OTHER PROBLEMS – HOW TO KEEP FROM BEING CHEATED

"He who knows a thousand works of art, knows a thousand frauds."
— Horace

"Art forgery is the most marvelous crime. Lots of money to be made without penalty."
— Thomas Hoving, former director of the Metropolitan Museum of Art

"If you wish to enjoy the subtleties of deceit, seek them all in the revelations of art imitation—one cannot fail to be amused at the clever shrewdness of the master thief when the fraud is revealed."
— Louisine Havemeyer, collector

FORGERIES HAVE TAKEN PLACE for thousands of years. Every type of object—paintings, sculpture, books, furniture, tapestries, china—has been forged at one time or another. Apparently even Michelangelo was not immune to such matters. According to legend, when the great Renaissance sculptor showed Lorenzo de' Medici a cupid he had just completed, Lorenzo commented, "If you put it in the ground, I'm sure it would pass for an ancient work." The cupid eventually was sold as an antique to a cardinal.

There are so many fakes and forgeries that some experts believe they equal the real things in number. A distinguished museum director once claimed that about forty percent of all the works he examined were forgeries, misattributed or so doctored by restorers that they ceased to be what they had been originally. This ratio is probably increasing because the market has become big business. As collectors give their choicest pieces to our museums and works are lost to natural disasters such as fires, floods and earthquakes—and to the eternal greed of men—the supply of fine objects shrinks and the demand for them rises. The relics of ancient civilizations in South America were looted and then melted down by the Spaniards. In Central Africa, a firm excavated thousands of ancient gold ornaments and melted them down for their gold content. These actions serve to stimulate frauds and thefts.

This chapter offers a brief review to illustrate how easily one may be taken in by dishonest and irresponsible persons. "Forewarned is forearmed."

The Vatican laid claim to much of Europe because of a forged document known as the Donation of Constantine.

The Piltdown man forgery was made of the skull of an Australian aborigine and the jawbone of an orangutan.

Hitler never wrote his diaries. Howard Hughes never wrote his autobiography.

Lillian Russell's ruby ring was a fake. Judge Roy Bean would have shot himself had he known.

Half of the Salvador Dali prints on the market are not his. Because there are so many fake Dalis, Christie's and Sotheby's will no longer handle them. The United States Post Office auctioned off about eleven thousand Dali prints that they had seized earlier. They went for $347,000.

Fakes of Maxfield Parrish paintings are also plentiful. Lawsuits and insurance settlements have followed some of the transactions, to no one's satisfaction.

A portrait of Mark Twain alleged to be by Anders Zorn fooled a major auction house, as did a fake Botero.

Occasionally a counterfeiting ring is caught red-handed. It took the FBI, Interpol and the Postal Department seven years to finally send to jail a family who was dealing in phony Dali, Chagall, Miró and Picasso prints. The swindlers were sentenced to serve thirty-three months.

A thief stole the Bible Concordance, dating from 1521, from the Adams Historic Site in Quincy, Massachusetts. It was recovered later in a camper's backpack. He had stopped at his health club for a workout before going to a commune.

A George Inness painting was stolen from a private school in New Hampshire. The police found it in the home of one of the state's assistant attorney generals. One never knows these days.

The Brooklyn Bridge, the Eiffel Tower and Trajan's Column in Rome have all been sold to gullible and unsuspecting people by con artists.

Even as unlikely a place as a golf course may be the site of fraud and chicanery to the unsuspecting collector. In 1997 four men were arrested at the world-famous Masters golf tournament in Georgia for selling fake autographs of the golf stars. Seventy thousand dollars worth of phony autographs were confiscated. The crooks were turned in by agents for Tiger Woods and Arnold Palmer. The FBI states that 70 percent of sports autographs are fakes.

Rome became known as "The Capital of the Fake" in the waning days of the empire.

Christians behaved badly during the Middle Ages, creating all kinds of fakes. Even the histories they recorded were found to be erroneous in many cases, altered to denigrate enemies. On the other hand, the Church hoarded and hid treasures to keep them safe from the barbarians. And the monks were responsible for saving the skills of reading and writing, which would have been lost had they not preserved and maintained manuscripts and documents.

The original *St. Francis and Brother Leo Meditating on Death* by El Greco is worth $2.5 million. A near-identical copy sold for $32,000. It is very difficult to tell them apart. Now dealers are openly trading in acknowledged copies.

When foreign governments started to restrict the export of their objects, the forgers had a field day. The fact that a collector could no longer buy and bring to America Old Master works of art from Italy made these objects more desirable. The able forger set out to appease the market.

Even the greatest museums have been fooled from time to time. The Metropolitan, the Louvre, the Getty and the National Gallery have all acquired objects that later turned out to be other than they had thought. These include would-be Rembrandts, Vermeers, Gainsboroughs and Daumiers and Greek, Roman and Egyptian antiquities. This was not because museum officials were careless or lacked knowledge and experience but because tests for authenticity depend on human judgments and humans can be wrong—not just museum professionals but outside, independent experts they call upon to certify acquisitions. Another factor is that new information is constantly being uncovered and may become known only after an acquisition has been made. And experts have been known to change their opinions with time, as was the case with the great scholar Bernard Berenson. We should not be too critical of misjudgments in the past. Rather, we should prepare ourselves to be as guarded and alert and attentive as possible in our personal searchings.

Out of this chaotic scene arise opportunities for forgers. Legitimate restoration is necessary in many instances. After all, man-made objects start to deteriorate as soon as they are completed. However, there are unscrupulous restorers who set out to alter the original in order to increase its value. This is not acceptable.

Broken statues are repaired and sold as whole pieces. They can be fairly recent pieces that have been artificially aged and since their provenance has been lost, the seller can create his own history for the piece. Jewelry can be pieced together using some old and some new, i.e., a necklace employing old beads but new gold settings that have been aged or gold covering a lead base.

In 1977, Italian authorities uncovered a long-running fraud operation involving dealers, restorers and auction-house employees. Fraudulent sales had apparently taken place, some for a million dollars and more. The perpetrators used old typewriters and museum stamps, falsified signatures and created false documentation. They had been carrying on this scam for two decades before being detected. The fallout will be with us for years.

Sometimes even forgers make names for themselves. One of the most famous forgers of all time, Hans Van Meegeren, created fake Vermeers and sold them to Hermann Goering. We might not call that a crime today; however, he also sold one to a leading Dutch museum for $5 million. For this he was tried and sent to prison for a year. He had left an interesting trail. From 1937 through 1945, several "lost" Vermeers suddenly appeared. All had been forged by Van Meegeren, who had developed a rather elaborate procedure. He would buy old, quite worthless paintings, those with cracks in them preferred. This condition is called "craquelure." He would then remove much of the old paint, leaving only enough to preserve the cracks. The canvases, also being old, helped deceive experts into believing that the paintings were, indeed, from the dates suggested by Van Meegeren. He developed a process to harden the new paint he applied to make it appear centuries old. If after all of this doctoring the cracks were not evident enough, he would simply roll the canvas back and forth so as to create new cracks in weakened spots.

Geovanna Bastianini created false ancient terra cotta busts, one of which was acquired by a major museum for an exceedingly high price. Even the most highly regarded expert can be fooled.

Alceo Dossena, "King of Forgers," was an Italian forger of classical, medieval and Renaissance sculpture in stone and terra cotta. He added patina by immersing his stone works in an acid concoction. He damaged his works purposely to make them look old. Dealers placed orders with him, then sold his creations as old and valuable pieces. Dossena was exposed when he sued a dealer for paying him so little and turning around and selling the same piece for a small fortune. Greed still does one in.

Elmyr de Hory, a Hungarian master forger, actually had a dealer to represent his fakes. He copied Matisse and Dufy, and the dealer, Legros, created phony provenances. The forger made some money and ended up in jail. The dealer made a fortune.

Otto Wacker, a Berlin dealer, offered for sale thirty-three Van Goghs. They were certified by a recognized art historian in 1927. Other experts began to question their authenticity. One by one they were led back to Wacker. He said he had purchased them from a Russian immigrant but could not reveal the seller's identity for security reasons. Eventually, Wacker went to trial and was found guilty of fraud.

Rembrandt has been copied so often that of the 558 pictures attributed to him at one time in 1906, his real works now number about 300. The Metropolitan Museum of Art counted among their collection 42 Rembrandts at their peak but now lists only 20. This is so surprising that the museum held a special exhibition displaying both authentic works and copies so as to explain to the public the differences.

Neither are auction houses and dealers without their share of deceptions. Unprincipled dealers have been known to join together to "fix" auctions. They agree in advance that they will not bid against each other, having selected the objects each is most interested in. This holds prices down and cheats the seller and auction house. This practice is called "bid-rigging" or "bid-pooling." This is an illegal procedure. In 1997, the Justice Department launched a wide-ranging anti-trust investigation of several New York dealers. They have subpoenaed financial records from the suspected dealers and the auction houses. If wrongdoing is proved, this would be a major scandal.

Vigilance against theft and forgery is always necessary.

Fakes, Forgeries, Stolen Goods, Copies and Other Problems

Even presumed strokes of luck may prove to be costly to the collector. One collector felt he had made a rare find when he purchased a painting at an auction in 1989. It was in poor condition. When he had it restored, he found it to be a more valuable painting than at first believed, and he sold it at auction for a much higher price than he had paid for it. With that the FBI entered the scene, having determined that the painting had been stolen in 1960. The FBI seized the object and returned it to its rightful owner. The collector suffered a total loss on his original purchase price and the cost of restoration.

Since ancient times, theft has posed as large a problem as fraudulence to both collectors and institutions alike. If ever there was a case for the "a stitch in time saves nine" philosophy, protecting your collections is it.

Romans removed art treasures from cities they conquered and brought them to Rome as early as the third century B.C. In 189 B.C. a Roman general brought 785 bronzes and 230 marble statues to Rome from a Greek city. In the time of Caesar, foreign pieces flooded Rome. Private citizens formed their own museums. Caesar's collection of cameos was famous. Everything came to Rome—gold, silver, manuscripts, tapestries.

Grave robbers have always done a lively business, going back to the Egyptian Pharaohs. Today they plunder cemeteries for statues, columns and benches that bring high prices as garden decorations.

Looting by victorious armies has taken place since the beginning of history. From the Renaissance on, rulers have considered art legitimate plunder. The sacking of Rome in 1527 led to art treasures being "exported" to the Austrian National Museum. The Swedish National collection contains art looted during the religious wars. The British Parliament participated in this game. They sold at auction the art collection of King Charles I after beheading him.

These acts often destroy the history of the object so it becomes increasingly difficult, if not impossible, to establish its

145

authenticity. For example, British troops looted the Summer Palace in Peking, China in 1860; great quantities of Chinese art surfaced in England and Europe in the years following. It is nearly impossible to this day to determine the origin and source of many of these works of art.

During the French Revolution and the Napoleonic Wars an orgy of looting took place. Mobs destroyed royal residences, and their glorious belongings went with the winds. During the Napoleonic Wars, long trains of wagons carried to Paris art treasures from Italy, Austria, Germany, the Low Countries and Spain. Even the Vatican surrendered a hundred works of art for removal to the Louvre. Milan and Parma were plundered and their treasures shipped by sea to Marseilles. Napoleon's generals raided castles, private homes and estates and walked off with what they wanted. The balance was spread out among courts, public arenas and favorites of the government. Toward the end of Napoleon's reign, the Louvre overflowed with objects from all of Europe. The Allies who finally defeated him did their best to return the stolen objects to their rightful owners, but it was an extremely difficult task. One of Napoleon's most notable thefts was of the four larger-than-life horses from the San Marco Palace in Venice. Exact copies will be looking down on you on your next visit to Venice; the originals, having been returned by the Allies, are safeguarded within the palace.

A couple of anecdotes from the Napoleonic Wars may bring a smile to the reader. Many treasures the French gathered in Egypt and shipped to France were intercepted by Lord Nelson at the Battle of Trafalgar, where the English fleet destroyed the French fleet. The English recovered these objects and they now form the core of the great collection in the British Museum. Napoleon never received them! Neither did Napoleon wind up with the fifteen-foot-tall nude statue of himself that the Duke of Wellington found in the basement of the Louvre; in a bit of turnabout, the duke had it transported to his London residence, where it stood in stark display.

One official count reported that five thousand objects were returned to some nineteen powers that Napoleon had defeated. Of course, much was lost, having been misappropriated and put away in places unknown to people who had no knowledge of their worth, provenance or how to care for them. Works keep emerging after decades, even centuries, of having been "lost." Their provenance is difficult, if not impossible, to ascertain. When they reappear on the market today, it is easy to be misled.

During World War II, the Nazis looted all of the countries they conquered. One of the most valued and treasured was the famed Amber Room taken by the Nazis from the palace of Catherine the Great and installed in a German castle in East Prussia. As the Russians advanced, it was disassembled, to be shipped deeper into Germany. That is the last known of it. It has simply disappeared. New hope has arisen, though, as two pieces of exquisite furniture that were in the Amber Room have surfaced in the hands of Germans who claim they inherited them. They may eventually lead to uncovering the fabulous Amber Room after a half-century.

In all, it is estimated that more than 60,000 objects were removed from Europe during the war, taken either from or by their rightful owners; 22,000 works of art were shipped from France alone and delivered to Germany. Modern art was discarded or sold in Switzerland. Perhaps a third of all of the art in France was purloined. Most were taken from Jewish owners and marked "Property of the Third Reich." Hitler had plans for a museum of European art to be built in Austria. After the war, art stolen from Austrian Jews was auctioned off for $14.5 million and the proceeds returned to surviving family members. This investigation is apt to go on for years. Much of the art the Nazis absconded with has disappeared, as have its original owners.

The tale relating to the collection of the Rothschild barons is one of many dramatic stories of art in the war. The Rothschild collection was first offered for sale in 1921; that sale was canceled because of a sudden fall in currency values. Ten years later, the collection was again offered—and once again withdrawn, this time because of the Depression. Then, in 1941, Hitler confiscated the entire collection. It was finally returned at the close of the war.

A French government report stated that nearly two thousand works, including paintings by Monet, Renoir and Gauguin, now in French museums and public buildings, including the Louvre, may have been stolen by the Nazis from Jewish owners. Hector Feliciano, the author of *The Lost Museum: The Nazi Conspiracy To Steal the World's Greatest Works of Art*, estimates that the locations of twenty thousand works stolen by the Nazis are still unknown, although most of them undoubtedly rest in museums of private collectors' homes.

An exhibition staged a few years ago by a major museum, which drew hundreds of thousands, apparently exhibited several paintings stolen by the Nazis. They had been purchased later by a Swiss industrialist. The entire matter is now under investigation.

A trustee of a major museum is being sued by a German citizen who claims the trustee bought a Degas pastel that had been stolen from the German's family by the Nazis. The trustee is free of any guilt but may lose his purchase price and the painting. The matter is in the courts.

In 1939, before Germany invaded, the Polish government took extraordinary precautions and managed to spirit many art treasures out of Poland, routing the works through Romania to France and then England for the final trip by steamer to Canada. The Nazis took everything that was left.

After the war the Allies appointed "monument men," whose assignments were to locate confiscated objects and return them to their rightful owners. Much was accomplished; they performed miracles under the conditions that existed. Still, many objects were lost and more had been destroyed. Authorities keep trying to locate treasures and return them to their owners. This effort has been complicated by the fact that as they advanced into Germany, the Russians destroyed much that they came across, including castles, churches and museums. That loss will never be calculated. Thousands of works that were shipped back to Russia are only now surfacing, having been treated as a closely guarded state secret all these post-war years. Although a few pieces have recently been returned to Germany, the Russian legislature has passed legislation "nationalizing" these looted objects as part payment for the ruin Germany wreaked on Russia.

The same old problems remain. Who owns these pieces? Are they authentic? How much remains unknown? This adds to the difficulties faced by modern collectors. Can they be certain that the objects they are being offered are indeed not only what they are said to be, but that the seller has the right to offer them to the collector and that the collector, in turn, is protected legally?

This decade is no exception. A Kuwaiti returned to his home after Saddam Hussein's armies had been driven out to find his house and safe rifled of every piece of his valuable collection of ancient Arabic art. His records were destroyed as well. He determinedly started calling auction houses, museums and dealers in an attempt to reconstitute his inventory. He is following leads. Some pieces have been sold at auction; others are in dealer's hands, but the dealers tend to insist on high payments for their return. It will take a tremendous amount of time, energy and money to locate his treasures.

Theft poses as large a problem to institutions as it does to individuals. The theft of books from libraries is a national and international pestilence. Stephen Carrie Blumberg stole $20 million worth of rare books from 268 libraries over two decades. He was turned in by his best friend for the $56,000 reward. A Spanish husband of a Harvard student stole books valued at $750,000 from Harvard libraries. He was planning to ship them to his home in Spain for resale when he was detected. A former student at the University of California at Los Angeles was sentenced for a $1 million theft. A history professor at Ohio State University raided its libraries for rare documents. A man known as the "slasher" cut rare books to shreds to obtain certain pieces at Northwestern University. The head of Boston College's rare book collection was caught stealing many volumes and offering them for sale through a major auction house, which turned him in. A Vietnamese computer expert in Germany was caught with more than five thousand books on specialized nonfiction subjects that he had stolen from libraries. He had so many crammed into his apartment that he barely had space for a bed. These cases dramatize how careful book collectors must be.

A senior vice-president of a New York Stock Exchange company pleaded guilty to embezzling over $12 million to pay for antique clocks he collected. Time finally ran out for him. He'll have to pay $3 million in taxes, too.

The largest art theft in the United States took place at the Isabella Stewart Gardner museum in Boston in 1990. Two men dressed as policemen entered the museum, shut off the security system, bound two guards and walked out with masterpieces by Rembrandt, Manet, Vermeer, Degas and others. They have yet to be found, despite a $1 million award. Now the frustrated trustees have increased the reward to $5 million. The case is complicated by the fact that no insurance was in force, the reason being that Mrs. Gardner's will stipulated that absolutely nothing could be changed within the museum. The trustees reckoned they needn't bother with insurance because they could never replace anything stolen or damaged with other art work without breaking her will.

New York and Los Angeles have become the art theft capitals of the world. The Los Angeles Police Department has a specialist dealing with stolen art. The Art Loss Register in New York reports a dramatic rise in theft since the middle 1980s. They have eighty thousand stolen works of art on file, with more than ten thousand in the past year alone. Only a small percentage of stolen objects is ever returned to the owner.

Thieves frequently steal objects for ransom. Insurance companies would rather pay a fraction of an object's worth as ransom than to pay full value to the insured. This is a primary reason to insure with a reputable company. The insurance company will work overtime to have your valuable object returned unharmed.

The recitation of a famous case will illustrate this point. Though it occurred decades ago, it could have happened yesterday. Pinkertons, the famous detective agency, felt that a certain Adam Worth was one of the most remarkable criminals they had ever encountered. An American who lived in London, Worth stole millions of dollars worth of art, jewelry, and cash over four decades. His most celebrated crime was his theft of the Gainsborough portrait of the Duchess of Devonshire from the premises of one of the most reputable London art dealers. The Duchess was a distant relation of Princess Di. The portrait had been purchased at a Christie's auction by an art dealer. It was literally a second-story job, with Worth shinnying up a wall to an open window on a foggy London night, cutting the painting out from its frame and exiting the same way. Twenty-five years later, with Pinkertons acting as go-between, Worth returned the *Duchess* to the dealer for a ransom sum, which, while large, was far less than the actual value of the painting. The exchange took place in Chicago. In 1905 J. P. Morgan acquired the picture for $150,000. Worth's biography has recently been published, entitled *The Napoleon of Crime*.

Patriotism can be a motivation in theft. The most famous thief of all time, the Italian Vincenzo Perugia, stole the *Mona Lisa* from the Louvre because he claimed it really belong to Italy where Leonardo had lived and painted. He was sentenced to prison for seven months, and the painting was returned to the Louvre, where it still hangs, now behind glass.

The famous painting of the Duke of Wellington by Francisco Goya was lifted from the National Gallery in London. Over the next five years, the thief sent several written messages to the authorities instructing that funds be paid to charitable organizations in return for the painting. Each time his demands were refused. Eventually, a frustrated truck driver turned himself in.

Since the painting was returned unharmed and the jury believed his motivation was noble, he received a short sentence of three months.

Works are constantly being smuggled into the United States. The collector who buys an object that has been illegally exported from a country is subject to having the object returned and/or facing an expensive and embarrassing lawsuit. Smugglers are clever. An anecdote from Lord Joseph Duveen's experience illustrates the lengths to which some will go. An owner advised Duveen that he had a valuable painting for sale—a small but fine *Crucifixion*. When the seller arrived in London from Italy, he displayed a much larger and quite ordinary painting. Duveen, shocked, explained that this was not the painting he had been expecting. The seller smiled and carefully removed the back of the large painting. There, hidden behind the picture, was the painting Duveen wanted. The seller had used this method to smuggle it out of Italy. It was sold by Duveen at that time to an American collector for $50,000. Years later in 1929, Duveen bought the same painting at auction for another collector for $375,000.

Very probably matters of this nature were handled somewhat more loosely then than they might be today. Nevertheless, in 1909 Duveen was hauled into court by United States Customs for undervaluing imports of art and thus avoiding or reducing import duties. Duveen settled for a payment of $1.4 million, not an insignificant sum even now, nine decades later. In today's dollar, the fine would be many times this figure.

The practice of smuggling has not let up. In 1977, a leading auction house's agent in Milan apparently helped smuggle an eighteenth-century painting out of Italy for auction in London. The person was secretly filmed in his office allegedly discussing the deal. When asked by the seller if there was some way to get it out of the country, the employee said, "we can smuggle it out." The employee has been suspended while the event is being investigated. Even the finest lose their way at times. Remain on guard!

Fakes, Forgeries, Stolen Goods, Copies and Other Problems

It can be difficult to get title to well-known foreign objects even having purchased it directly from the owner or through a dealer. Recently the Getty Museum, eight months after having purchased an Old Master painting from the trustees of England's Howard Castle for $5.4 million, found the sale reversed. The painting ended up at the National Galleries of Scotland. United Kingdom export laws, created for the purpose of retaining national treasures in England, allow local funds to be raised so as to keep prized art works in Great Britain.

There are several steps the alert collector can take to protect him- or herself from the dangers of fraud and theft.

- Do business only with reputable people you know personally or by reputation. Insist that their statements regarding authenticity be in writing. If they are reluctant to do so, you should be reluctant to buy. Ask for references.
- Do your own research. While you may not ever become as knowledgeable as a dealer or museum curator, you will become aware of some of the pitfalls in your field of interest. This will allow you to ask relevant questions, which will, in turn, alert the seller that he is not dealing with an unknowing and uncaring amateur.
- Employ an advisor or graduate student to do some sleuthing for you. This will turn up important information and the cost will not be exorbitant.
- Get a second opinion, particularly if the object is of high value. Obtain a separate appraisal from someone other than the seller.
- When buying at auction, examine the catalogue carefully. The auctioneer has the responsibility of making his description accurate and complete. Also, understand before the bidding the guarantees the auction house offers regarding the works in which you are interested.
- Question the provenance and attributions. Authenticity of objects is of prime importance. Ask for scientific analysis where this is applicable. If you are careless and do not question this vital information, the seller may be relieved of any responsi-

bility in the future should the object you buy turn out to be other than you were led to believe.
- Consult competing galleries and auction houses. If anything is amiss, they will delight in letting you know.
- Don't be pressured by seller or time. Take your time and do your homework before buying.
- If the deal sounds too good to be true, then it probably is.

It is difficult to be too careful. Remember at all times that it is your money that is at stake. If you follow these suggestions, there is little you need fear. The forgeries will probably be revealed. The value of the piece can be ascertained with reasonable accuracy. The provenance will have been well established. Your rights will be understood by both by you and the seller.

Chapter 15

THE ECONOMICS – COLLECTING FOR PLEASURE AND PROFIT

"Art can be a lucrative investment."
— *Fortune* Magazine

"Invest in the art market? Soy beans might be safer."
— *Fortune* Magazine

VERY FEW COLLECTORS say that financial gains are their chief motivation or expectation. That does not mean that they are not sharp buyers, willing and able to negotiate with the best. Nor that they will not sell a particular object when they find it has appreciated greatly in value or that it no longer fits their collection objective. Even the museums sell from time to time, in order to use the funds to acquire new objects.

The examples offered below illustrate some remarkable instances of expanding values that demonstrate that there are ample opportunities for financial gain. However, it is wise to remember that values in all markets ebb and flow and collectors are subject to these same basic laws of economics. To get the most out of collecting, it is essential that the collector pursue an area of great personal interest.

Peter Watson, author of *From Manet to Manhattan*, presents a detailed, long-term analysis of art prices and the comparative financial returns from other investment opportunities. Watson's conclusions are for the art market alone; data may well lead to different results for other markets such as coins, stamps, antiques, classic cars and hundreds of other collectibles. He came to three conclusions.

First, in the long term, art as an investment performs about half as well as other investments. He describes the difference as "the price of pleasure." Second, there are periods of "art booms" when some real money can be made if you are fortunate enough to buy low and sell high. And finally, of late, since World War II, the rate of return has been higher. Watson attributes this in part to a better-educated public with greater appreciation of the arts as well as to the auction houses, which are making art more available to more people.

In summary, Watson seems to feel that if money is all one is interested in, invest elsewhere. But there is no way to measure the value of the pleasure collecting can bring. That is an individual matter.

The main thrust of Watson's book, echoed by many collectors, is that one should collect not for money alone but for pleasure, education and posterity. This way you will be guaranteed the most fabulous returns imaginable.

And if you follow the rules for successful collecting in Chapter 5, your chances of having financial success as well will be considerably enhanced.

All collecting categories are created by collectors. First occurs a major category such as stamps. Then collectors begin to discriminate and organize subdivisions. Stamp collectors can concentrate on stamps from the British Empire; from Europe; from the United States; first day covers only; and so forth. Once the categories are established by collectors, they create the "rarities"—those objects within a category or subdivision that are fewest in number. How collectors categorize objects becomes all powerful, all controlling. Collectors determine which categories are most valuable and "correct." Thus markets are established. As categories grow, groups of collectors publish journals, price guides, and form clubs and organizations. These activities feed the category and stimulate the market.

Following are some brief reportings that are not only of interest in themselves but may help with understanding the market, its practices and values.

The first great European paintings were decorative works done in the thirteenth century by Duccio di Buoransegna. Others followed—by Leonardo, Breughel the Elder and Bellini in the fifteenth and sixteenth centuries; Titian, Rubens, Van Dyck and Rembrandt in the sixteenth and seventeenth; Caneletto, Hogarth, Gainsborough and Fragonard in the eighteenth; Van Gogh and Gauguin in the nineteenth and Turner, Cézanne, Monet, Renoir and Degas in the early twentieth century. Today it is estimated that the majority of the works by these artists are held by public institutions and each year several more enter these institutions. Virtually the entire known output of Leonardo, Michelangelo and Raphael are owned by public institutions. This trend will continue as the number of museums increase, the existing museums continue to expand and institutions such as the Getty buy up the world's best for the people. Small wonder prices for these irreplaceable treasures keep mounting, It's the old capitalist system working at its best by responding to supply and demand.

Artists seem to leave larger estates than writers, actors or composers. Painters are the most highly paid of all artists. When Picasso died in 1973 at age ninety-one, his estate was valued at $250 million (paintings, sculpture, ceramics, prints, drawings). Picasso paintings sold at auctions alone have exceeded $400 million. The Impressionists were not as prolific. Sisley averaged twenty-seven canvases a year, Manet ten and Degas nine per year.

A Van Gogh painting set the world record price when his *Dr. Gachet* portrait sold for $82.5 million. Yet he was able to sell only one painting in his lifetime, even though his brother was an art dealer. Now many paintings previously attributed to Van Gogh are being proclaimed frauds.

Vermeer, whose magnificent paintings are among the most treasured and sought after by museums and private collectors alike, never sold a painting in his lifetime.

The top price Jackson Pollock received for one of his works while alive was $5,340. Now his paintings go for millions.

Rembrandt, one of the world's greatest artists and a recognized genius whose paintings sell for millions today, died bankrupt. He was also a collector of paintings, armor, bronzes, medals and drawings.

A 1910 baseball card featuring Honus Wagner sold for $640,000 in 1996 at a Christie's auction. It was a promotion for Piedmont cigarettes at the time of issue.

The uniform worn by Lou Gehrig, the New York Yankees' great first baseman from the 1920s and 30s, for his farewell speech at Yankee Stadium went for $306,130 at a 1997 auction.

The Russian jeweler Fabergé created exquisite jeweled Easter eggs for the Russian czars and czarinas in the late nineteenth and early twentieth centuries. He made fifty in all, of which forty have survived. Because of their beauty and rarity and having been made for Russian royalty, they now sell for millions of dollars each. In 1989, one was auctioned off by Christie's for $3.1 million. In 1994 another went for $5.6 million.

The Beatles had a heyday at a recent auction. Paul McCartney's guitar went for $202,955. His birth certificate fetched $73,064. John Lennon's velvet cape captured $227,602. In all, nearly three hundred items were auctioned off for $1.46 million.

In England, Prince William, second in line for the British throne, has had his name tags purloined from his underwear briefs. His fellow students at the private school he attends apparently believe they will be of considerable value if and when he becomes king.

To the other extreme, sixty years after Bonnie and Clyde were mowed down in a police ambush in Louisiana, members of their families auctioned some personal items including Clyde's bullet-riddled shirt. It was valued at $40,000 but sold for $85,000. This was more money than they ever got from a bank holdup!

For Jackie Kennedy Onassis's auction, Sotheby's sold 125,000 catalogues. Catalogue sales alone amounted to $2.5 million, which went to the John F. Kennedy Foundation. The four-day auction grossed $34.4 million, seven times the estimate of $4.5 million. As an example of the prices bidders were willing to pay for Kennedy possessions, Arnold Schwarzenegger paid $772,500 for President Kennedy's MacGregor golf clubs and bag.

A ninety-year-old teddy bear that belonged to the late King Frederik of Denmark went for $44,700. It was found in the attic of the royal castle.

The Duchess of Windsor's jewels, many given her by her husband, the former king of England, sold for $50 million in 1987—well above estimates.

A 197-year-old bottle of Madeira wine fetched $23,000 at a Sotheby's auction. It had been owned by Thomas Jefferson.

A cabinet owned by the Duke of Windsor brought $717,000.

Porcelain china made for Chinese Chairman Mao Ze Dong sold for $1 million at a 1996 auction. This was for the reserve pieces only, not the china from which he personally dined. That is kept in a museum.

Old Hollywood movie posters sell for large amounts. The first auction of this type of material took place in Beverly Hills in 1989. Now there are dozens of such auctions held every year. At a Sotheby's auction in 1997, a poster for *The Mummy* starring Boris Karloff sold for $410,000; in all, there were 380 posters auctioned off. Private sales are probably higher.

Clark Gable's Oscar, won in 1934 for *It Happened One Night*, sold for $607,000 at Sotheby's auction in 1996. The previous high was $563,500 paid for the Oscar that Vivien Leigh won in 1939 for *Gone With the Wind.* "Rosebud," the sled Citizen Kane had as a child, captured $233,500 at a Christie's auction. Marilyn Monroe's dresses (one went for over $50,000), a lamp from Rick's Café in *Casablanca* and Rudolph Valentino's make-up kit have all appeared at auction. The trade in Hollywood collectibles is so big that Christie's has opened a Beverly Hills sales office.

When Paul Mellon started buying British art in volume, the prices of some works of art increased 1,000 percent.

John Singer Sargent's painting of a niece sold for $11.1 million at a Sotheby's auction in 1996. This was a record price for an American painting. The previous high for a Sargent was $7.6 million in 1994.

In 1996, six paintings exceeded $10 million each at auction. Others undoubtedly went for this much and more at private sale.

The Getty Museum bought the 1509 painting *Rest on the Flight into Egypt with St. John the Baptist* from a private owner for $22.5 million.

Rare books can be a sound investment. A first edition of F. Scott Fitzgerald's *The Great Gatsby,* with dust-jacket, published in 1925 has an estimated value of $20,000 to $30,000.

Bill Gates, America's wealthiest individual, purchased Leonard da Vinci's *Leicester Codex* manuscript for $30.8 million about ten years after Armand Hammer acquired it for around $4 million.

A privately published copy of *Peter Rabbit* went for $48,300 at auction. An autographed manuscript of the Sherlock Holmes mystery *The Sign of Four* brought $519,500.

Comic books have grown in value. An expert states, "If you had put $1,000 into the right books in 1982, you would have done better than somebody who put $1,000 into stocks, despite the bull market." This is not true of all comic books, of course. The valuable books today are those from the "golden" and "silver" ages—the 1930s and 1940s. Superman issues from then could go for $25,000 at Sotheby's or Christie's. One premier Superman sold for $150,000. An introductory Batman went for $105,000. A pair of Archie comics went for $100,000. A collector paid $176,000 for the 1940 debut issue of Captain Marvel. The industry Bible is the *Official Overstreet Comic Book Price Guide*, which list thousands of titles.

There is a tremendous boom in price guides for collectibles. Forty years ago there were fewer than sixty books on collectibles; now more than nine hundred are published each year and some six thousand collectible books and guides are now in print. Many are not sold through bookstores but at fairs and sales only.

A sixteenth-century helmet found in an attic fetched $250,000 at auction. A 65 million-year-old fossilized skeleton of a Tyrannosaurus Rex found by Sue Hendrickson while taking a walk on a Texas ranch owned by Maurice Williams sold for over $8 million at Sotheby's; the Field Museum of Natural History was the buyer.

The Vatican is now marketing copies of its art treasures. Catholic schools will receive 40 percent of the gross proceeds, the Vatican will receive 5 percent and John Connelly, the promoter, 5 percent (the remaining 50 percent covers the cost of the goods). Reproductions include angel ashtrays, Vatican art neckties, plaster reproductions of God's finger touching Adam's from the Sistine Chapel. Incidentally, the Vatican Library has thousands of items still not catalogued–there's no telling what is apt to show up in the future.

The Shelbourne Museum in Vermont was forced to sell some of its art holdings, including Impressionists, Old Masters and American paintings and sculpture, due to shaky finances. Sotheby's was selected because it guaranteed the museum in excess of $20 million, which meant the auction house, not the museum, took the risk. The twenty-two works offered for sale delivered $29.94 million to the museum, so Sotheby's had their guarantee covered. A Degas bronze of a ballerina sold for $11.9 million. The works garnered premium prices in part because of their provenance: they had been given to the museum by the founder, Electra Havemeyer Webb, daughter of the great collectors and benefactors of the Metropolitan Museum, the H. O. Havemeyers.

More mundane items also bring in high amounts. One example is the collecting of Coca-Cola bottles. This has become so popular that there is an illustrated guidebook on Coke bottles and specialized dealers now ply the trade. President Jimmy Carter is a collector.

Furniture and other decorative objects often appreciate with time. The Rhode Island Desk and Bookcase by the Townsend and Goddard families of Newport is one of only ten examples of this unique American piece of furniture. The last one remaining in private hands was sold at Christie's in 1989 for $12.1 million.

A single straight-back wooden dining room chair designed by the architect Frank Lloyd Wright sold for $70,000 at auction. A friend of mine, who sold it, told me he had bought four of them years ago at a garage sale for $5 each. Previously he had given one to a local museum and his wife received two when they were divorced—still a pretty good return on his initial investment. More recently, an oak chair also designed and built by Wright sold for 131,428 British pounds (about $220,000) to the Victoria and Albert Museum in England. Hope my friend didn't notice this.

A royal silver Louis XV tureen sold for $10.3 million at Sotheby's.

The two largest auction houses are now publicly owned. You can buy shares of stock in them. Sotheby's is listed on the New York Stock Exchange. The stock is largely owned by Americans, and an American, Alfred A. Taubman, is chairman. Christie's has a narrow over-the-counter stock offering, largely in England. This testifies to how large the auction business, which caters to collectors, has become. In 1996, Christie's sales were

$1,602,000,000 and Sotheby's $1,599,595,000—a virtual standoff. Because of the increases in sales and activities, both of the major houses find they must now expand their space in New York. Christie's is doubling its space with a move to Rockefeller Center.

Museums now float bond issues. The Museum of Modern Art in New York City, the third museum to do so, has been so successful it receives ratings from Moody's for the bonds it issues.

Financial analysts write about collectibles as investments. Some have outpaced the stock market. *Forbes* magazine, a leading business journal, runs a regular column on collectors. *The Wall Street Journal* reports on sales by the leading auction houses.

There is a mutual fund for speculating on art.

The Smithsonian Institution, our largest museum complex, the basic operation of which is entirely funded by the Federal government, has employed Hollywood's number one talent agency, Creative Artists Agency, to help them market the Smithsonian and its many products. The agency represents stars such as Tom Cruise, David Letterman, Meryl Streep, Steven Spielberg and author Michael Crichton. This illustrates how important marketing to the public has become to our museums.

Fine objects have a way of being misplaced or squirreled away where they are then forgotten. This can happen in the highest of places. It was in London's National Gallery that Lord Kenneth Clark, the director, came upon "some twenty rolls of canvas, thick with dust, which I took to be old tarpaulins." They were actually paintings by the great English artist J. M. W. Turner, one of which, *Seascape: Folkestone*, sold for over $10 million in 1984.

A retired couple bought an old picture frame at a New England flea market. When they took it apart, they found two paintings hidden behind the main picture, which made it the biggest discovery in American folk art. Hannah Cohoon's *Tree of Light* done in 1845 and Polly Collin's *Gift Drawing*, 1854, are Shaker watercolors. Sotheby's will auction them for an estimated $300,000.

In Praise of America's Collectors

It is almost impossible to believe this story. Levi Leitner purchased a watercolor and then forgot about it. One hundred years later it was discovered resting behind a door in Leitner's home. Experts determined it to be a James Whistler painting. In 1997 it was sold at auction for $123,000. Have you looked behind your doors lately?

Or this tale of new treasures recently discovered. Not long ago a large batch of drawings, watercolors and sketches by the artist Camille Pissaro were found in the former home of the painter Frederick E. Church. For some reason no one knew they were there or how they ever entered his house. In an analogous way, an 1883 Van Gogh drawing was rediscovered in 1995. Previously the drawing had not been attributed to the artist, but experts from the Van Gogh Museum in Amsterdam revisited and declared it now a Van Gogh. It had been in a private collection for three generations.

It is wise to remember that taste, judgment and values can change from generation to generation. Lord Elgin brought the Elgin marbles from the Parthenon in Greece to England and offered them for sale to the British Museum. The marbles were dismissed at the time as being inferior. Nevertheless the British government did reluctantly agree to acquire them from Elgin at half his asking price. He was so desperate that he accepted the paltry offer even though his original asking price represented only half of his total costs in retrieving them. Today they are priceless.

Watches have a special attraction. There are five great watchmakers whose products obtain highest value—Patek Philippe, Rolex, Vacheron and Constantine, Audemars Piquet (all Swiss) and France's Cartier. In 1996 a unique platinum Patek Philippe wrist watch sold for $1.6 million. A stainless steel Patek Philippe wrist watch sold for $863,000. One reason Patek Philippe attains the highest prices is that it easy to check the origin of each watch. Since founded in 1839, the company has numbered each watch and can offer complete information to a buyer. Values increase if a watch has had a famous owner.

Stamps have the highest sales volume of any collectible. Americans buy $200 million of new stamp issues each year. These are for collecting purposes only—not for use as postage—and represent a huge windfall for the Postal Department. Stamp dealers report that there are several kinds of stamp collectors. One is the topical collector—someone who collects on a single subject such as space exploration or Disney characters. Another grouping is those who collect tagged stamps. These stamps are treated chemically so that they glow under ultra violetlight. Others look for freak stamps that have errors. There are classic early issues, first day issues, stamps from certain countries or from certain periods. An example is the stamp-collecting rage that took place in Hong Kong. With the British relinquishing their rule after 132 years, stamp collectors furiously bought the last stamps issued by the British government and the first stamps issued by the new Chinese government. In the collecting world, first and last day of issue are particularly desirable.

Stamps can achieve tremendous values. A rare Swedish stamp, the Treskilling Yellow printed in 1855, is prized for its yellow-orange color, which is regarded as a printing error and is unique among the other greenish stamps in this issue. It was recently purchased by an anonymous buyer for $2.3 million.

The Dawson cover, mailed from Hawaii to New York, sold to a collector for $6,000 in 1905 and for $2,090,000 in 1995. The envelope contains a charred portion. It was found in a furnace and retrieved just before being burned up.

King George V of England and his cousin Czar Nicholas of Russia were both avid stamp collectors. King George's collection remains at Buckingham Palace. The whereabouts of Nicholas's collection is unknown.

Rare coins grow in value every decade. Not long ago an 1804 silver dollar, one of fifteen in existence, sold at auction for $1.8 million. It topped the previous record of $1.4 million paid for a 1913 liberty nickel, only five of which are known to exist. Collecting coins can lead to a lifetime of joy and value.

There is also money in old cars. The Volkswagen Beetle, introduced in America in 1949, is now a collector's item. In good condition it will sell for $12,000. Classic cars are those built from 1929 through 1939, the Depression years. It is best to collect cars that were expensive when new. On a car's twentieth anniversary, it starts appreciating. Therefore, the propitious time to buy an old car is when it is eighteen or nineteen years old.

A 1949 Ferrari 166MM Barchetta sold for $1,652,500 at Christie's Pebble Beach auction in 1996. Another collector paid $7 million for a 1930s Blower Bentley race car.

More than 160 classic antique bicycles from the former Schwinn bicycle museum are being sent to auction by the new owners. Values are expected to be very high.

American art objects and antiques may frequently be purchased at lower prices in Europe because they are not appreciated as much there. It is difficult to find American objects in any English or European museum. They are not accepted. The same general principle applies to buying German pictures in Italy, etc.

Large paintings are less desirable in a country of small houses, such as Holland. Religious objects are in less demand in Protestant countries and with many collectors.

Antiques one hundred years old and older are not subject to import duties by United States customs service. Antiques grow in value, whereas modern reproductions are less likely to.

The Internal Revenue Service has a special advisory committee to review art donated to charities as well as estate and gift-tax valuations. In 1995 it accepted 49 percent of the declared values and disagreed with 47 percent. The rest required further analysis. In the previous year, the IRS accepted 47 percent and disagreed with 53 percent. It examines about $150 million worth of gifts each year. The IRS is toughest on estate and gift-tax evaluations: it accepted 60 percent of charitable contribution appraisals but only 45 percent of estate and gift-tax valuations.

We should always be reminded that values change. When the first shipments of gold and silver art treasures from the

Americas arrived in Spain, they were judged to be among the greatest ever created. Before the sixteenth century drew to a close, these same treasures were being melted down for their gold and silver content.

The "Pantin Silkworm" paperweight was purchased in the 1920s for $59 and then sold for $3,000 at auction in 1953. It was then purchased by a dealer for King Farouk of Egypt. However, the day of the auction, Farouk abdicated and the dealer was left with the object. It next appeared in 1983 when the great collector Arthur Rubloff paid $143,000 for it at a Sotheby's auction. Rubloff subsequently gave his collection to the Art Institute of Chicago, where it is on permanent exhibition.

Art appreciation, including collecting, has become so popular and active that a new $1.4 billion gambling palace planned for Las Vegas will feature in its gambling halls $60 million worth of contemporary art.

A wooden cigar store Indian, late nineteenth century, went for $29,900 at a 1996 Christie's auction.

A Tiffany leaded glass lamp brought $431,000 at Christie's in 1995.

The British Rail Pension Fund, of all things, decided to invest in the art market. Its advisors had determined through research that many categories of art had been good investments over time. They have proved to be right so far, as some of the art has been sold.

James Herrals, the superintendent at Watergate at the time of the notorious break-in, kept the lock that had been picked by the burglars and sold it at auction for $13,000.

"Pickers" cruise our country, often on the back roads, looking for objects of value that may be tucked away in people's homes, small antique shops and garage sales. When found, they buy at the lowest price possible and then resell them to larger dealers and collectors. This is a full-time occupation for many, who travel tens of thousands miles a year in their pursuit of lost and neglected treasures.

As this book goes to print, Christie's announced a new world record for a single-owner auction—$207,165,298 for the sale of Victor and Sally Ganz's collection. The Ganzes bought their first painting in 1942. Picasso's erotic portrait of his mistress, painted in 1932, sold for $48,402,500. It is never too late.

Chapter 16

Things That People Collect – from Advertising to Zodiacs

"Is there anything somebody doesn't collect?"
– Robert MacNeil, MacNeil-Lehrer Report

"My husband will buy anything from a pyramid to the tooth of Mary Magdalene."
– Mrs. J. P. Morgan (The tooth, appropriately presented, is in the Metropolitan Museum of Art)

THE PUBLIC INTEREST in collecting has grown. Americans have started collecting a wide and diverse variety of objects from fine art to decorative objects to advertising ephemera. Museums have had to increase the number of their departments as the range of collectibles expands.

Collecting collectibles has exploded. Fewer than sixty books on collectibles existed forty years ago. Now over six thousand are in print. *Kovel's Antique and Collectibles Price List* sells 100,000 copies a year at $15.00 a copy. There are price list books for almost anything and everything—arrowheads, Coca-Cola bottles, chewing tobacco tins—even plastic dinnerware. They can be found at dealers' and fairs—wherever collectibles are being sold. Now the international auction houses Sotheby's and

Christie's are getting into the act. Both recently introduced a series of collectibles' guides.

All of the items listed here are subject to serious collecting by many collectors. Lest you feel some may be too inconsequential to merit listing, it may be of interest to know that a major museum received and accepted as a gift twelve thousand bubble gum wrappers and regularly schedules exhibitions of costumes and gowns; that the New York Botanical Garden has a special exhibit of miniature trains, including authentic reproductions of structures; that the University of Indiana accepted a gift of some sixteen thousand miniature books; and the Art Institute of Chicago has a stunning collection and permanent exhibition of paperweights, left to the museum by one of its trustees. The Chicago museum also has a handsome permanent exhibition of the world-famous miniature Thorne rooms, which were created and contributed to the museum by Mrs. James Ward Thorne. The Santa Barbara Museum of Art has a special collection of dolls that is regularly exhibited. Presidents George Washington, Thomas Jefferson and John Adams all collected marbles (the kind you play with). Christie's offers nine large, illustrated books on watches alone.

The lesson here is that you can be as inventive and daring as you choose to be. You may find inspiration as you read through this list. It is far from exhaustive. There are more not listed than listed.

Advertising specialties	Antique typewriters
American cut glass	Apple peelers
American Indian art	Armor
American silver	Arrowheads
Ancient glass	Art catalogues
Animals (taxidermy)	Artificial eyes
Antique jewelry	Automobile emblems
Antique medical instruments	Automobiles
Antique trunks	Barbed wire

Baskets
Beer bottles
Beer signs
Bibles
Bird eggs
Bird houses
Black Americana
Bookmarks
Books
Brass ware
British Royal memorabilia
Bubble gum wrappers
Butterflies
Butter pats
Buttons
Calendars
Calling cards
Cameras
Candlesticks
Canes
Ceramic head vases
Charts
Chewing tobacco tins
Children's books
Christian Dior dresses
  and gowns
Christmas ornaments
Cigarette trading cards
Cigars
Cigar cutters, lighters
  and bands
Cigar store Indians
Clocks
Coca-Cola ads
Coca-Cola bottles

Coins
Collages
Comic strips
Commemorative plaques
Corkscrews
Costume jewelry
Costumes
Cracker Jack prizes
Cut-glass decanters
Daggers
Decorative arts
Decoys
Doll houses
Dolls
Dresses
Drinking cups used
  by famous people
Duck stamps
Embroidered handkerchiefs
Enamel boxes
English cartoons
English silver
Early American tools
Etchings
Exotic plants
Fabrics
Fairground art
Farm implements
Figureheads (as on ship prows)
Figurines
Fine scientific instruments
Firefighter hats
Fireplace equipment
First Ladies' gowns
Fishing lures

171

Fishing tackle
Flashlights
Fountain pens
Frames
Fruit jars
Furniture
Games
Garden tools
Glass
Golf balls
Golf books
Golf clubs
Golf scorecards
Golf tees
Guns
Haitian Voodoo art
Hand tools
Hat jewels
Hatpins
Hollywood memorabilia
Horseless carriages
Ice skates
Indian relics
Inkwells
Insects
Ivory carvings
Jazz
Jewelry
Juke boxes
Kitchen utensils
Knitting and crochet
  equipment
Lanterns
Letters
Limited editions

Locks and keys
Lunch boxes
Maps
Matchbook covers
Matchbooks
Medals
Medical antiques
Military uniform
Miniature books
Miniature rooms and furniture
Model trains
Motorcycle memorabilia
Mugs
Nautical antiques
Needlework
Netsukes
Newspapers
Paintings
Paper money
Paperweights
Pebbles
Perfume bottles
Petroleum collectibles
Pews
Pewter
Phonograph records
Photographs
Pinball machines
Pistols
Plastic dinner ware
Playing Cards
Poison bottles
Political campaign memorabilia
Portrait miniatures
Portraits

Posters
Pottery
Pressed glass
Radios
Railroad memorabilia
Railroad timetables
Razors
Replicas of animals
Rocks
Rugs
Rustic furniture
Salt cellars
Scientific glassware
Scrimshaw
Sculpture
Shawls
Shaving mugs
Shells
Shoes
Silhouettes
Silver Certificates
Silver plate
Snowshoes
Souvenir metal buildings
Space collectibles
Spanish architecture
Spittoons
Spoons
Stamps
Stock certificates
Swords
Tarzan artifacts
Teddy bears
Telephones
Texaco signs
Thimbles
Tiaras
Tie clasps and stickpins
Ties
Tiffany
Toasting forks
Tokens
Toys
Trading cards
Trucks
Ukuleles
Vacuum cleaners
Valentines
Victorian treasures
Walking sticks
War memorabilia
(Civil, Revolutionary, etc.)
Watches
Watch keys
Weather vanes
Whistles
Wooden sleds
Wooden tennis racquets
Wood turnings
World's Fair memorabilia
Wristwatches
Yiddish materials
Zodiacs

Chapter 17

PREDICTIONS – THOUGHTS FOR A NEW MILLENIUM

"For I dipt into the future as far as human eye could see, saw the vision of the world and all the wonders that would be."
— Alfred, Lord Tennyson

"What of our values and heritage will we carry with us? And what gifts will we give to the future?"
— William Jefferson Clinton, 42nd President of the United States

SINCE THE NATION'S COLLECTORS have been so generous in donating their holdings to museums for the benefit of all, it is easy to chart the course that collecting in America has taken in the past. More challenging, perhaps, is to envision what the future will bring to the subject. With the dawn of a new century, even a new millennium, the temptation to look forward is inescapable. Following are some musings on the future of collecting nationally and internationally.

More of the world's greatest art treasures will leave the public market and become institutionalized. Others will be lost or destroyed. The market for the remaining cultural objects in the public arena will continue to be very active—particularly the market for objects from the sixteenth to twentieth century. The value of fine art and other cultural objects will increase—it's a simple case of supply and demand.

The production of new art will boom. There will be no shortage of new art and new products for collectors. As the number of objects considered "collectible" increases, the number of collectors will grow dramatically. African Americans and members of other ethnic groups will expand their interest in collecting and supporting museums. Collecting will go global: people of all nations will participate.

The new fortune-makers will continue the practice established by the great collectors in the past and assemble collections which will eventually become part of our museum system for the benefit of the people. Thus the number of museums and their size will continue to increase.

To service this boom in collecting, auction houses will continue to grow and offer an even wider range of objects. Art schools and museums will start offering courses on collecting. Many new career opportunities will occur in the collectible and museum fields.

In the future, the Internet will play an ever larger part in bringing information on cultural affairs to the public. Already there are online data bases that help collectors locate objects and assess the marketplace. As our affairs and dealings become more global, legal problems will expand. Prices will fluctuate as the economy and tax structure change.

"Lost" treasures of art will continue to be uncovered and rediscovered.

The importance and necessity of conservation will grow. It is becoming a moral and physical imperative.

Appendix

Institutions Named for Collectors

In response to generous contributions of collectors, many institutions elect to name themselves after the collector, recognizing the vital importance of private collections to the launching. Similarly, one of the strongest motivations for collecting is to establish for all time one's name as a contributor to humankind's well-being and betterment. Nothing can be more rewarding to both the collector-donor and the people. Our cultural and educational systems would not exist in their present forms and excellence without these very generous and farsighted individuals. Take a moment to read this list and quietly thank each donor for enriching the lives of all of us. There is nothing comparable in the world today.

The institutions are listed in alphabetical order. The full name of the collector-donor follows the name and location of the institution which is identified with the donor's last name only to facilitate the alphabetical listing. While the list is long, it is meant to be only representative, not complete. There are far more institutions founded by and named for collectors than are listed here, and the ranks grow every year. It is interesting to note how many are established in small towns as well as in our largest cities.

Ackland Art Center, Chapel Hill, North Carolina—William Hayes Ackland
Albright-Knox Art Gallery, Buffalo, New York—James Albright and Seymour Knox
Aldrich Museum of Contemporary Art, Ridgefield, Connecticut— Larry Aldrich
Alf Museum, Claremont, California—Raymond M. Alf
Allen Memorial Art Museum, Oberlin, Ohio—Dr. Dudley Peter Allen
Allen Textile Collection, Madison, Wisconsin—Helen Louise Allen
Allyn Museum, New London, Connecticut—Lyman Allyn
Anderson House, Anchorage, Alaska—Oscar Anderson
Ashby Museum, Copper Center, Alaska—George I. Ashby
Astor Library, New York City—William B. Astor
Autry Western Museum, Los Angeles, California—Gene Autry
Barnes Foundation, Merion, Pennsylvania—Dr. Albert C. Barnes

Barnum Musuem, Bridgeport, Connecticut—P. T. Barnum
Bass Museum of Art, Miami Beach, Florida—John and Johanna Bass
Bellingrath Gardens & Home, Theodore, Alabama—Walter Duncan Bellingrath
    and Bessie Morse Bellingrath
Benton Museum, Storrs, Connecticut—William Benton
Biggs Museum, Dover, Delaware—Sewell C. Biggs
Bily Museum, Spillville, Minnesota—Frank and Joseph Bily
Block Gallery, Northwestern University, Evanston, Illinois—Mary and Leigh Block
Bohart Museum, Davis, California—R. M. Bohart
Bowdoin College Museum of Art, Brunswick, Maine—James Bowdoin
Bowman Museum, Princeville, Oregon—A.R. Bowman
Brest Museum, Jacksonville, Florida—Alexander Brest
Brown House Museum, Denver, Colorado—Molly Brown
Brown Library, Providence, Rhode Island—John Carter Brown
Bryant Museum, Tuscaloosa, Alabama—Paul W. Bryant
Buck Museum, Tonkawa, Oklahoma—A. D. Buck
Bullen Gallery, Arcata, California—Reese Bullen
Burns Museum, Van Buren, Arkansas—Bob Burns
Burritt Museum, Huntsville, Alabama—William Henry Burritt
Butler Institute of Art, Youngstown, Ohio—J. G. Butler, Jr.
Carnegie Institute Museum of Art, Pittsburgh, Pennsylvania—Andrew Carnegie
Carnegie Libraries (3,000)—Andrew Carnegie
Carter Museum of Western Art, Fort Worth, Texas-—Amon Carter
Charles and Emma Frye Museum, Seattle, Washington—Charles and Emma Frye
Chrysler Museum of Art, Norfolk, Virginia—Walter P. Chrysler
Claremont McKenna College, Claremont, California—Donald C. McKenna
Clark Institute, Williamstown, Massachusetts—Sterling and Francine Clark
Colburn Gallery, Burlington, Vermont—Frances Colburn
Cooper-Hewitt Museum (Smithsonian Institution), New York City—
    granddaughters of Peter Cooper
Copley Library, La Jolla, California—James S. Copley
Corcoran Gallery of Art, Washington, D.C.—William Wilson Corcoran
Cozens Ranch, Winter Park, Colorado—William and Mary Cozens
Crandall Musuem, Canterbury, Connecticut—Prudence Crandall
Crear Library, Chicago, Illinois—John Crear
Crocker Art Museum, Sacramento, California—E. B. Crocker
Crown Center for Health, Hinsdale, Illinois—Robert Crown
Crown Gallery, Art Institute of Chicago, Illinois—Henry Crown
Currier Gallery, Manchester, New Hampshire—Moody Currier
Cushing/Whitney Medical Library, New Haven, Connecticut—
    Harvey Cushing and John Hay Whitney
Eastman House, Rochester, New York—George Eastman
Ellis Museum, Abiquiu, New Mexico—Florence Hawley Ellis
Fetterman Museum, Fort Valley, Georgia—A. L. Fetterman
Field Museum of Natural History, Chicago, Illinois—Marshall Field

Appendix

Flagler Museum, Palm Beach, Florida—Henry M. Flagler
Fleischer Museum, Scottsdale, Arizona—Donna H. Fleischer
Folger Shakespeare Library, Washington, D.C.—Henry Clay Folger and
 Emily Jordan Folger
Ford Museum & Greenfield Village, Dearborn, Michigan—Henry Ford
Forney Transportation Museum, Denver, Colorado—Jack D. Forney
Fowler Museum, University of California, Los Angeles—Francis Fowler
Fox Museum, Dillingham, Alaska—Samuel K. Fox
Francis Museum, Jacksonville, Alabama—Dr. James C. Francis
Freer Gallery of Art (Smithsonian Institution), Washington, D.C.—
 Charles Lang Freer
Frick Art Center, Pittsburgh, Pennsylvania—Henry Clay Frick
Frick Collection, New York City—Henry Clay Frick
Fullerton Museum Center, San Bernardino, California—Robert V. Fullerton
Gardner Museum, Boston, Massachusetts—Isabella Stewart Gardner
Getty Center, Los Angeles, California—J. Paul Getty
Gibbes Museum of Art, Charleston, South Carolina—James Schoolbred Gibbes
Gilcrease Institute of American History and Art, Tulsa, Oklahoma—
 Thomas Gilcrease
Gilmore Art Center, Kalamazoo, Michigan—Genevieve and Donald Gilmore
Governor Ross Plantation, Seaford, Delaware—Governor William Ross
Grey Museum, Lackawaxen, Pennsylvania—Zane Grey
Guggenheim Museum, New York City—Solomon R. Guggenheim
Hammer Museum, Los Angeles, California—Armand Hammer
Harman Art Museum, Pagosa Springs, Colorado—Fred Harman
Harrah's Automobile Museum, Reno, Nevada—William Harrah
Hartung Automotive Museum, Glenview, Illinois—Lee Hartung
Harvard University, Cambridge, Massachusetts—John Harvard
Heard Museum, Phoenix, Arizona—Dwight B. and Marie Bartlett Heard
Hearst Castle, San Simeon, California—William Randolph Hearst
Hearst Museum of Anthropology, Berkeley, California—Phoebe Apperson Hearst
Heckscher Museum, Huntington, New York—August Heckscher
Heller Nature Center, Highland Park, Illinois—Walter E. Heller
Hendrickson House Musuem, Wilmington, Delaware—Andrew Hendrickson
Herbert Institute, Augusta, Georgia— Gertrude Herbert
Higgins Armory Museum, Worcester, Massachusetts—John Woodman Higgins
High Museum of Art, Atlanta, Georgia—Mrs. Joseph M. High
Hirshhorn Museum and Sculpture Garden (Smithsonian Institution),
 Washington, D.C.—Joseph R. Hirshhorn
Houghton Library, Harvard University, Cambridge, Massachusetts—
 Arthur A. Houghton, Jr.
Hunter Museum of Art, Chattanooga, Tennessee—George Hunter
Huntington Library, Art Gallery, and Botanical Gardens, San Marino,
 California—Henry E. Huntington
Jackson Museum, Weaverville, California —J. J. Jackson

Jackson Museum, Sitka, Alaska—Dr. Sheldon Jackson
Johnson Museum, Ithaca, New York—Herbert F. Johnson
Johnston Museum, Kingston, New York—Fred J. Johnston
Karpeles Library, Santa Barbara, California—David Karpeles
Kaye Museum of Miniatures, Los Angeles, California—Carole and Barry Kaye
Kent Museum, Philadelphia, Pennsylvania—Atwater Kent
Kimbell Art Museum, Fort Worth, Texas—Kay Kimbell and Velma Fuller Kimbell
Kirkland Musuem, Denver, Colorado—Vance Kirkland
Kislak Foundation, Miami Lakes, Florida—Jay I. Kislak
Kohl Children's Museum, Wilmette, Illinois—Dolores Kohl
Krannert Art Museum, Champaign, Illinois—Mr. and Mrs. Herman Krannert
Kreeger Museum, Washington, D.C.—David Lloyd Kreeger
Lehman Pavilion, Metropolitan Museum of Art, New York City—
	Philip and Robert Lehman
Leu Garden, Orlando, Florida—Harry P. Leu
Luthy Botanical Garden, Peoria, Illinois—George L. Luthy
Lynn Museum, Hurricane Mills, Tennessee—Loretta Lynn
Mathews Museum, Sanibel, Florida—Bailey Mathews
McAllister House Museum, Colorado Springs, Colorado—
	Major Henry McAllister
McCormick Museum, Wheaton, Illinois—Robert R. McCormick
McMillan Museum, Brewton, Alabama—Thomas E. McMillan
McNay Art Institute, San Antonio, Texas—Marion Koogler McNay
Magnes Museum, Berkeley, California—Judah L. Magnes
Manilow Sculpture Park, University Park, Illinois—Nathan Manilow
Mark Twain Memorial, Hartford, Connecticut—Mark Twain
May Natural History Museum, Colorado Springs, Colorado—John May
Meadows Collection, Southern Methodist University, Dallas, Texas—
	Hurtle Meadows
Meeker Home Museum, Greely, Colorado—Nathan Cook Meeker
Mercer Museum, Doylestown, Pennsylvania—Henry Mercer
Michener Galleries, Austin, Texas—James A. Michener
Michener Museum, Doylestown, Pennsylvania—James A. Michener
Miller Museum, Sitka, Alaska—Isabel Miller
Milliken Museum, Los Baños, California—Ralph Milliken
Mitchell Flight Museum, Milwaukee, Wisconsin—General Billy Mitchell
Mitchell Museum of Western Art, Trinidad, Colorado—A. R. Mitchell
Nelson-Atkins Museum, Kansas City, Missouri—William Rockhill Nelson
	and Mary M. Atkins
Nelson Gallery, Davis, California—Richard L. Nelson
Neuberger Museum, Purchase, New York—Mr. and Mrs. Roy R. Neuberger
Newberry Library, Chicago, Illinois—Walter Loomis Newberry
Norton Gallery, Palm Beach, Florida—Mr. and Mrs. Ralph Norton
Page Museum, Los Angeles, California—George C. Page
Page Museum, Wasilla, Alaska—Dorothy G. Page

Appendix

Paneak Museum, Anaktuvuk Pass, Alaska—Simon Paneak
Patton Museum, Chiriaco Summit, California—General George Patton
Peale Museum, Baltimore, Maryland—Rembrandt Peale
Peter Museum, Santa Rosa, California—Jesse Peter
Peterson Automobile Museum, Los Angeles, California—Robert Peterson
Phillips Collection, Washington, D.C.—Duncan Phillips
Pierpont Morgan Library, New York City—J. Pierpont Morgan
Plotkin Judaica Museum, Phoenix, Arizona—Sylvia Plotkin
Pritzker Gallery, Art Institute of Chicago, Illinois—Pritzker family
Regenstein Library, University of Chicago, Illinois—Joseph Regenstein
Remington Art Museum, Ogdensburg, New York—Frederic Remington
Ringling Museum of Art, Sarasota, Florida—John and Mable Ringling
Rockefeller Folk Art Center, Williamsburg, Virginia—Abby Aldrich Rockefeller
Rogers House Museum Gallery, Taos, New Mexico—Millicent Rogers
Rogers Park, Palisades, California—Will Rogers
Rogers-Evans Museum, Victorville, California—Roy Rogers and Dale Evans
Rosenbach Foundation Museum, Philadelphia, Pennsylvania—Philip H. and
    A. S. W. Rosenbach
Russell Museum, Great Falls, Montana—Charles M. Russell
Ryerson Library, Art Institute of Chicago, Illinois—Martin Ryerson
Sackler Gallery, Metropolitan Museum of Art, New York City, New York—
    Arthur B. Sackler
Selby Gardens, Sarasota, Florida—Marie Selby
Simon Museum, Pasadena, California—Norton Simon
Skirball Cultural Center, Los Angeles, California—Jack and Audrey Skirball
Slaughter Ranch Museum, Douglas, Arizona—John Slaughter
Sloan Museum, Flint, Michigan—Alfred P. Sloan, Jr.
Small Jewish Museum, Washington, D.C.—Lillian & Albert Small
Smart Museum of Art, University of Chicago, Illinois—David and Alfred Smart
Smith Museum of Art, Hayward, California—C. E. Smith
Speed Art Museum, Louisville, Kentucky—J. B. Speed
Stanford University Museum of Art, Palo Alto, California—Leland Stanford, Jr.
Stewart Museum, Indiana, Pennsylvania—James Stewart
Strawn Art Gallery, Jacksonville, Illinois—David Strawn
Strong Museum, Rochester, New York—Margaret Woodbbury Strong
Taft Museum, Cincinnati, Ohio—Taft Family
Telfair Academy of Arts and Sciences, Savannah, Georgia—Telfair Family
Terra Museum of American Art, Chicago, Illinois—Daniel J. Terra
Thompson Arboretum, Superior, Arizona—Boyce Thompson
Thorne Mansion, Milford, Delaware—Parson Thorne
Timken Art Gallery, San Diego, California—Timken Family
Tinker Swiss Cottage Museum, Rockford, Illinois—Robert H. Tinker
Tweed Museum, Duluth, Minnesota—George P. Tweed
Ulrich Museum, Wichita, Kansas—Edwin A. Ulrich
Vaile Museum, Palmer Lake, Colorado—Lucretia Vaile

Volck Museum, Watsonville, California—William Volck
Wadsworth Atheneum, Hartford, Connecticut—David Wadsworth
Walker Art Center, Minneapolis, Minnesota—T. B. Walker
Walters Art Gallery, Baltimore, Maryland—William and Henry Walters
Watson Library, Metropolitan Museum of Art, New York City—
 Thomas J. Watson
Webster Historical Society, West Hartford, Connecticut—Noah Webster
Weir Farm Historic Site, Wilton, Connecticut—J. Alden Weir
Weisman Museum, Malibu, California—Frederic R. Weisman
Weyerhauser Museum, Little Falls, Minnesota—Charles A. Weyerhauser
Whitney Museum, Hamden, Connecticut—Eli Whitney
Whitney Museum of American Art, New York City—
 Gertrude Vanderbilt Whitney
Widener Library, Harvard University, Cambridge, Massachusetts—
 Harry Elkins Widener
Winterthur Museum, Winterthur, Delaware—Henry Francis du Pont
Ziff Jewish Museum, Miami Beach, Florida—Sanford L. Ziff

Bibliography

Alsop, Joseph. *From the Silent Earth: A Report of the Greek Bronze Age*. New York: Harper & Row, 1964.
Alsop, Joseph. *The Rare Art Traditions: The History of Art Collecting and Its Linked Phenomena Wherever These Have Appeared*. New York: Harper & Row, 1982.
Auchincloss, Louis. *J.P. Morgan: The Financier as Collector*. New York: Abrams, 1990.
Bachmann, Konstanze, ed. *Conservation Concerns: a Guide for Collectors and Curators*. New York: Cooper-Hewitt National Museum of Design, Smithsonian Institution; Washington, D.C.: Smithsonian Institution Press, 1992.
Basbanes, Nicholas A. *A Gentle Madness: Bibliophiles, Bibliomanes, and the Eternal Passion for Books*. New York: H. Holt and Co., 1995.
Behrman, Samuel Nathaniel. *Duveen*. New York: Random House, 1952.
Blumay, Carl. *The Dark Side of Power: The Real Armand Hammer*. New York: Simon & Schuster, 1992.
Brown, Milton Wolf. *The Story of the Armory Show*. 2nd edition. New York: Abbeville, 1988.
Burnham, Sophy. *The Art Crowd*. New York: D. McKay Co., 1973.
Burt, Nathaniel. *Palaces for the People: A Social History of the American Art Museum*. Boston: Little, Brown, 1977.
Cabanne, Pierre. *The Great Collectors*. London: Cassell, 1963.
Caplin, Lee Evan, ed. *The Business of Art*. Englewood Cliffs, N.J.: Prentice-Hall, 1982.
Carlin, John. *How To Invest in Your First Works of Art: A Guide for the New Collector*. New York: Yarrow Press, 1990.
Carmichael, Bill. *Incredible Collectors, Weird Antiques, and Odd Hobbies*. Englewood Cliffs, N.J.: Prentice-Hall, 1971.
Clark, Kenneth. *Another Part of the Wood: A Self Portrait*. New York: Harper & Row, 1974.
Clark, Kenneth. *The Other Half: A Self Portrait*. New York: Harper & Row, 1977.
Clotworthy, William G. *Homes and Libraries of the Presidents: An Interpretive Guide*. Blacksburg, Va.: McDonald & Woodward, 1995.
Conservation Research 1995. (Volume 51, *Studies in the History of Art*) Washington, D.C.: National Gallery of Art; Hanover, N.H.: Distributed by the University Press of New England, 1995.
Constable, William George. *Collectors and Collecting*. New York: Art Treasures of the World, 1954.
Cooper, Douglas, ed. *Great Family Collections*. New York: Macmillan, 1965.

Cooper, Douglas, ed. *Great Private Collections*. London: Weidenfeld and Nicolson, 1963.

Davis, Nancy. *Handle with Care: Preserving Your Heirlooms*. Rochester, N.Y.: Rochester Museum & Science Center, 1991.

DeGregorio, William A. *The Complete Book of U.S. Presidents*. New York: Dembner Books; Distributed by W. W. Norton, 1984.

Duveen, James Henry. *Collection & Recollections: A Century and a Half of Art Deals*. London: Jarrolds, 1935.

Eagle, Joanna Shaw. "Artists as Collectors," *Art in America,* vol. 55, no. 6, November - December 1967, pp. 55 - 63.

Ellis, Margaret Holben. *The Care of Prints and Drawings*. Nashville, Tenn.: AASLH Press, 1987.

Encycolpedia of Art, Vo. 4. New York: McGraw Hill, 1961.

Esterow, Milton. *The Art Stealers*. New York: Macmillan, 1966.

Feliciano, Hector. *The Lost Museum: The Nazi Conspiracy To Steal the World's Greatest Works of Art*. New York: Basic Books, 1997.

Fowles, Edward. *Memories of Duveen Brothers*. London: Times Books, 1976.

Getty, J. Paul. *The Joys of Collecting*. New York: Hawthorn Books, 1965.

Getty Museum, J. Paul. *The J. Paul Getty Museum*. Malibu, Calif.: J. Paul Getty Museum, 1975.

Gingrich, Arnold. *Business and the Arts*. New York: Paul S. Erikson, 1969.

Gosling, Nigel. *The Adventurous World of Paris, 1900 - 1914*. New York: W. Morrow, 1978.

Greenwood, Douglas McCreary. *Art in Embassies: Twenty-five Years at the U.S. Department of State, 1964 - 1989*. Washington, D.C.: Friends of Art and Preservation in Embassies, 1989.

Guggenheim, Peggy. *Out of This Century: Confessions of an Art Addict*. New York: Universe, 1979.

Guldbeck, Per E. *The Care of Antiques and Historical Collections*. With revisions, an introduction, a chapter on photographs, and an index by A. Bruce MacLeish. 2nd edition, revised and expanded. Walnut Creek: AltaMira Press, 1995.

Haas, Irvin. *Historic Homes of the American Presidents*. New York: D. McKay, 1976.

Hale, Nancy. *Mary Cassatt*. Garden City, N.Y.: Doubleday, 1975.

Havemeyer, Louisine W. *Sixteen to Sixty: Memoirs of a Collector.* New York: Ursus, 1993.

Hoving, Thomas. *False Impressions: The Hunt for Big-time Art Fakes*. New York: Simon & Schuster, 1996.

Hoving, Thomas. *Making the Mummies Dance: Inside the Metropolitan Museum of Art*. New York: Simon & Schuster, 1993.

Hughes, Robert. *Nothing If Not Critical: Selected Essays on Art and Artists*. New York: Knopf, 1990.

Jones, Cranston. *Homes of the American Presidents*. New York: McGraw-Hill, 1962.

Le Vane, Ethel and J. Paul Getty. *Collector's Choice: The Chronicle of an Artistic Odyssey Through Europe*. London: W. H. Allen, 1955.

Lipman, Jean, comp. *The Collector in America*. New York: Viking, 1970.

Loria, Jeffrey H. *Collecting Original Art.* New York: Harper & Row, 1965.
MacNeice, Jill. *A Guide to National Monuments and Historic Sites.* New York: Prentice Hall, 1990.
Macintyre, Ben. *The Napoleon of Crime.* New York: Farrar, Straus and Giroux, 1977.
Mathews, Nancy Mowll. *Mary Cassatt: A Life.* New York: Villard Books, 1994.
Mellon, Paul. *Reflections in a Silver Spoon: A Memoir.* New York: W. Morrow, 1992.
Meyer, Karl Ernest. *The Art Museum: Power, Money, Ethics: A Twentieth Century Fund Report.* New York: Morrow, 1979.
Meyer, Karl Ernest. *The Plundered Past.* New York: Atheneum, 1973.
Muensterberger, Warner. *Collecting, an Unruly Passion: Psychological Perspectives.* Princeton, N.J.: Princeton University Press, 1994.
Museum of Fine Arts, Boston. *Museum of Fine Arts Boston.* (Series: Newsweek/Great Museums of the World) Boston: Museum of Fine Arts, 1969.
Naisbitt, John, and Patricia Aburdene. *Megatrends 2000: Ten New Directions for the 1990's.* New York: Morrow, 1990.
National Gallery of Art, Washington, D.C. *National Gallery, Washington.* (Series: Newsweek/Great Museums of the World) Washington, D.C.: National Gallery of Art, 1968.
Naude, Virginia Norton, and Glenn Wharton. *Guide to the Maintenance of Outdoor Sculpture.* Washington, D.C.: American Institute for Conservation of Historic and Artistic Works, 1993.
Nicholas, Lynn H. *The Rape of Europa: The Fate of Europe's Treasures in the Third Reich and the Second World War.* New York: Knopf, 1994.
Norton, Thomas E. *100 Years of Collecting in America: The Story of Sotheby Parke Bernet.* New York: Abrams, 1984.
Norton Simon Museum of Art at Pasadena. *Selected Paintings at the Norton Simon Museum, Pasadena, California.* New York: Harmony Books, 1980.
Pollack, Barbara. *The Collectors, Dr. Claribel and Miss Etta Cone.* Indianapolis: Bobbs-Merrill, 1962.
Preserving Our Heritage: A Review of the Conservation Needs and Resources in the Philadelphia Metropolitan Area. Philadelphia: William Penn Foundation, 1988.
Rees-Mogg, William, ed. *How To Buy Rare Books.* Oxford: Phaidon; Christie's, 1985.
Rinker, Harry L., Jr., ed. *Warman's Americana & Collectibles.* 7th edition. Radnor, PA: Wallace-Homestead, 1995.
Rush, Richard H. *Selling Collectibles for Profit & Capital Gain.* New York: Harper & Row, 1981.
Saarinen, Aline. *The Proud Possessors: The Lives, Times, and Tastes of Some Adventurous American Art Collectors.* New York: Random House, 1958.
Samuels, Ernest. *Bernard Berenson: The Making of a Connoisseur.* Cambridge, MA: Belknap Press, 1979.
Sandwith, Hermione, and Sheila Stainton, comps. *The National Trust Manual of Housekeeping.* Middlesex: Penguin Books in association with the National Trust, 1985.
Savage, George. *Forgeries, Fakes and Reproductions: A Handbook for the Art Dealer and Collector.* New York: Praeger, 1964.

Schultz, Arthur W., ed. *Caring for Your Collections.* New York: Abrams, 1992.

Secrest, Meryle. *Being Bernard Berenson: A Biography.* New York: Holt, Rinehart and Winston, 1979.

Secrest, Meryle. *Kenneth Clark: A Biography.* New York: Holt, Rinehart, and Winston, 1985.

Seligman, Germain. *Merchants of Art, 1800 - 1960: Eighty Years of Professional Collecting.* New York: Appleton-Century-Crofts, 1962.

Seligman, Germain. *Oh! Fickle Taste: Or, Objectivity in Art.* New York: B. Wheelwright Co., 1952.

Shelley, Marjorie. *The Care and Handling of Art Objects: Practices in the Metropolitan Museum of Art.* New York: Metropolitan Museum of Art; Distributed by Abrams, 1987.

Simpson, Colin. *Artful Partners: Bernard Berenson and Joseph Duveen.* New York: Macmillan, 1986.

Simpson, Mette Tang, and Michael Huntley, eds. *Sotheby's Caring for Antiques: The Complete Guide to Handling, Cleaning, Display, and Restoration.* New York: Simon & Schuster, 1992.

Snyder, Jill. *Caring for Your Art.* New York: Allworth Press; Saint Paul, Minn.: Consortium Book Sales & Distribution, 1990.

Spaeth, Eloise. *American Art Museums: An Introduction to Looking.* 3rd edition, expanded. New York: Harper & Row, 1975.

Taylor, Francis Henry. *The Taste of Angels: A History of Art Collecting from Rameses to Napoleon.* Boston: Little, Brown, 1948.

Tomkins, Calvin. *Merchants and Masterpieces: The Story of the Metropolitan Museum of Art.* New York: E. P. Dutton, 1970.

de Torres, Amparo R., ed. *Collections Care: A Basic Reference Shelflist; Based on the Collections Care Information Service, a Project of the National Institute for the Conservation of Cultural Property.* Washington, D.C.: The Institute, 1990.

Towner, Wesley, completed by Stephen Varble. *The Elegant Auctioneers.* New York: Hill & Wang, 1970.

Walker, John. *Self-portrait with Donors: Confessions of an Art Collector.* Boston: Little, Brown, 1974.

Ward, Philip R. *The Nature of Conservation: A Race Against Time.* Marina del Rey, CA: Getty Conservation Institute, 1986.

Wardell-Yerburgh, J.C. *The Pleasure of Antiques: Gold and Silver, Glass and Furniture, Pottery and Porcelain, Clocks and Watches.* London: Octopus Books, 1974.

Watson. Peter. *From Manet to Manhattan: The Rise of the Modern Art Market.* New York: Random House, 1992.

Wilson, William. *The Los Angeles Times Book of California Museums.* New York: Abrams, 1984.

Wittmann, Otto. *Art Values in a Changing Society; Revised from an Address; A Museum Director's View of the Art Market by Otto Wittmann before the London Financial Times Conference, New York, October 18, 1974.* Toledo, Ohio: Toledo Museum of Art, 1975.